How to Sous Vide

How to Sous Vide

EASY, DELICIOUS PERFECTION
ANY NIGHT OF THE WEEK

DANIEL SHUMSKI

Workman Publishing
New York

Library of Congress Cataloging-in-Publication Data

Names: Shumski, Daniel, author.
Title: How to sous vide : easy, delicious perfection any night of the week / Daniel Shumski.
Description: New York : Workman Publishing, 2021. | Includes index.
Identifiers: LCCN 2021027210 | ISBN 9781523512331 (paperback) | ISBN 9781523512331 (ebook)
Subjects: LCSH: Sous vide cooking. | LCGFT: Cookbooks.
Classification: LCC TX690.7 .S58 2021 | DDC 641.5/88--dc23
LC record available at https://lccn.loc.gov/2021027210

Design: Becky Terhune
Cover and interior photos: Waterbury Publications, Inc., Des Moines, IA
Photographer: Ken Carlson, Waterbury Publications, Inc., Des Moines, IA
Food Stylist: Joshua Hake
Food Stylist Assistant: Cassandra Monroe
Prop Stylist: Saley Nong
Author photograph: Alex Tran

Workman books are available at special discounts when purchased in bulk for premiums and sales promotions as well as for fundraising or educational use. Special editions or book excerpts can also be created to specification. For details, contact the Special Sales Director at specialmarkets@workman.com.

Workman Publishing Co., Inc.
225 Varick Street
New York, NY 10014-4381
workman.com

WORKMAN is a registered trademark of Workman Publishing Co., Inc.

Printed in the United States of America

First printing October 2021

10 9 8 7 6 5 4 3 2 1

Contents

CHAPTER 1

Sous Vide Basics

Though you may not have known it, you've probably had food cooked sous vide. Restaurants use it to cook food ahead of time and to perfection—helping to manage the last-minute scramble for orders—and the technique has gradually spread from there. Not long ago, sous vide equipment became accessible in price and in availability, with companies offering their gear to the home cook. The technique started in fine dining and has gradually expanded from rarefied kitchens to more humble eateries even to the coffee shop on the corner. And now to you.

Sous Vide Cooking in a Nutshell

How to describe sous vide cooking in a single breath: Food is sealed in a watertight package with the air removed and then cooked in a water bath at a precise temperature.

Okay, now a few more breaths: All of this is made possible by a device known as a sous vide circulator or immersion circulator, also called a "stick," "wand," or simply a "sous vide." The circulator is simple. It consists of a temperature gauge, a heating element, and a motor that pushes around the water for even heating.

Cooking sous vide means embracing reliable, replicable, and delicious results. We're talking meat that is cooked to astoundingly even perfection, where a steak done to medium is the same rosy shade from edge to edge. Sous vide cooking spares delicate seafood and vegetable dishes from overcooking.

While a lot of the buzz surrounding sous vide focuses on cooking meat—justifiably!—it also opens up a new supporting cast for your meals. Pasteurizing eggs sous vide (page 167) means not having to dither about raw eggs. Preparing bacon sous vide (page 62) and freezing it means cooked bacon is always easy and within reach. Infusing olive oil with chiles and vanilla (page 140) is such a great note with which to finish a dish.

And what about dessert? Cheesecake, ice cream, crème brûlée—enough said! (Okay, not quite enough said; see pages 194, 201, and 209.)

And maybe there's a misconception that sous vide cooking is complicated, possibly because it's unfamiliar or because it got its start in fancy restaurant kitchens. But in truth, it's easy. Once more for the people at the back: It's easy! Once you get over the gentle learning curve, you can do it in your sleep. (Perhaps literally if the recipe takes more than 8 hours.) This book shows you how and, even better, will show you why with recipes that highlight the best of sous vide cooking.

The Advantages of Sous Vide Cooking

PRECISION: Many sous vide circulators regulate temperature to within one-half of one degree Fahrenheit. Your oven can't manage that degree of precision. (Ovens might cycle within a band of 30°F, 40°F, or 50°F, and that's assuming they're even calibrated correctly in the first place.) Try setting a pot of water on the stovetop to, say, simmer at precisely 200.5°F; it won't happen. Sous vide's precision ties in nicely to the next point.

PREDICTABILITY: It's nice to have unpredictability in the sense of someone whisking you away on a surprise vacation. It's less nice to have unpredictability in the sense of overcooking your expensive steak, even though you thought you did it the same way as last time. Sous vide's precision and consistency combine to eliminate that room for error.

FORGIVENESS: Five more minutes won't matter. Ten more minutes won't matter either.

Half an hour? Eh, it probably won't matter. There aren't too many cooking methods that let you say that, but sous vide timing is very flexible. While food might start to break down and change texture after the recommended times, rarely will a short stretch of time be the make-or-break for dinner success. Try that with the pasta that turned to mush after 3 too many minutes or the pizza that burnt while you refreshed your social media feed. (That "like" was lovely. Was it worth a pizza?)

EASE: This is not just a lack of complication, though sous vide cooking is very straightforward once you know the deal. The ease also comes from the ability of the chef to deep-breathe and leave behind anxiety about dinner. Impressive results aside—for just a second—that's worth a lot, regardless of the cooking method.

TIME: While sous vide cooking can take a while—maybe a few hours, maybe more in some cases—that time is almost all passive. There's no watching, stirring, or poking involved. Sous vide cooking allows you to cook while you do the laundry or, um, write a cookbook.

NOVELTY: Look, you're interested in new cooking methods or you wouldn't be reading this. Since our cave-dwelling ancestors discovered fire and first submitted it to reviews from the cave public at large ("★not hot enough!"; "★too hot!"; etc.), there have only been so many new cooking methods. Sous vide qualifies.

PRACTICALITY AND PREPARATION: Sous vide cooking opens up possibilities for portioning and precooking. You have many options: Re-frigerate or freeze the sous vide cooked meat and then finish it later. Freeze portions of meat already seasoned and sealed, ready for their sous vide bath. (Yes, you can put the frozen and prepacked sous vide packets directly into the bath!) Get a jump on tomorrow's dinner or this weekend's barbecue by cooking a few chicken pieces for tonight and a few more later on.

IMPRESSIVENESS: Brag a little. You've earned it. When I mention I've cooked something using sous vide, the response is usually either "Who's that?" or "What's that?" Dinner isn't always for lingering and discussing, but if you want a talking point, sous vide delivers when everyone tastes the results and wants to know more. Or you can keep it a secret, and let everyone be wowed by your powers to cook a steak consistently and perfectly. I can see it going either way.

Is Cooking Sous Vide Safe?

Sous vide cooking is safe. But it's different from conventional cooking, and it flouts some of the rules we've learned as careful cooks. Let's take a closer look at the safety of sous vide.

Temperatures

Many of us have perhaps had certain food safety temperatures drilled into our heads. Do the temperatures 165°F for chicken, 160°F for ground beef, and 145°F for pork ring a bell? Those are the USDA's minimum recommended internal temperatures. (In the case of pork, with three minutes of resting time mandated.)

There is a very good reason for those temperatures—and a very good reason that they don't apply to sous vide cooking.

Those temperature benchmarks represent what I would call the "nuke from space" temperatures—those needed to instantly reduce bacteria to a safe level. Once the foods reach those temperatures, the USDA doesn't need to worry about how long the food has spent there; it's safe. The USDA simply does not expect that you will have a sensitive device regulating the cooking temperature to within one-half of a degree over the course of several hours. But you do! You have a sous vide circulator. So a new range of temperatures comes into play. The bottom line is that foods can cook at lower temperatures as long as they stay there for specified periods of time, and as long as they stay out of the temperature danger zone. For more details on this, see Sous Vide Food Safety (page 15).

SOUS VIDE BEST PRACTICES

Diligently follow the recipes and guidelines in this cookbook to stay safe. Here's what you're up against:

Some bacteria survive cooking by forming spores. Like the seed of a plant, when a spore is exposed to moisture, food, and an optimal temperature and environment, it will spring into action. Some types of bacteria can produce toxins that contaminate food. Many bacterial toxins cannot be destroyed by later cooking.

The bacteria of most concern for sous vide are the ones that form spores and those that multiply in warm conditions or in vacuum-packaged food. These include C. botulinum, which grows between 38°F and 113°F in vacuum-packaged foods, and C. perfringens, which grows between 39.2°F and 126°F.

• Sous vide cooking below 131°F—for seafood, for example—must never exceed 4 hours.

• Because of botulinum risk in vacuum-packed foods, all pouched foods, whether cooked or raw, must be stored at less than 37°F. The best way to do this is to store the pouched food between layers of ice in the back of the refrigerator. The maximum time to refrigerate pouched food is 2 days.

• If sous vide food is not served just after cooking, it must be cooled immediately. Place it in a mix of half ice and half water and replace the ice as it melts. The food should cool to less than 37°F within 2 hours. Store it in the refrigerator as directed above.

• The sniff test is not everything: When a vacuum is established, most organisms responsible for off-odors do not grow. But pathogens such as C. botulinum are of concern. Refrigeration—on ice, toward the back of the fridge, as specified above—must be below 37°F.

Source: *Guidelines for Restaurant Sous Vide Cooking Safety in British Columbia*, BC Centre for Disease Control

Plastics

Sous vide cooking often involves food sealed in plastic. "Plastic" is a broad term, so it's useful to specify the type of plastics we're talking about: polyethylene without plasticizers such as BPA.

Polyethylene in its solid form is not toxic and is approved for contact with food. (If it melts and you ingest it, that might be a different story. But we're not melting plastic here.) Many of the warnings about microwaving food in plastic or leaving plastic water bottles in the car (where they may heat up) center on concerns about the chemical BPA, which is not an issue with BPA-free polyethylene.

Ziploc-brand bags are typically made from polyethylene and state on the package that they contain no BPA. Generic varieties are also fine as long as the material is stated on the label. Freezer bags tend to be better suited because they're thicker and often have a double seal.

Vacuum-seal bags such as FoodSaver are also great for sous vide cooking. They are made from polyethylene, with a layer of nylon on the exterior. Again, check the label or ask the manufacturer to be certain.

Now, is it possible that more research will be done and different conclusions will be reached as to the safety of plastic for sous vide cooking? Absolutely. It's possible.

Here is how I reconcile that reality with my love of sous vide cooking:

With sous vide cooking's popularity at restaurants, I've almost certainly eaten food that's been cooked sous vide without my realizing it. So if I'm hoping to avoid it entirely, I've already lost on that count. In fact, when I look around me, I see a lot of plastic, in practically every room of my house, including the kitchen. (For more on the environmental impact of plastic and possible alternatives, see How to Choose and Seal Bags, page 13).

I also eat food that's been cooked over fire, a process known to generate carcinogens.

I don't offer this to justify taking a wild risk in cooking, just to place in context any risk that might exist.

Ultimately, there is a risk built into many things we eat. It's prudent to reduce the risks but unrealistic to eliminate them entirely. For my part, I have concluded that with proper precautions (such as paying attention to labels and temperatures) sous vide cooking is safe as part of a balanced diet.

One other piece of good news: If you're avoiding plastic entirely, there are a few other options for some foods. Glass canning jars and reuseable packets made from silicone (not a plastic) are available and suitable for many recipes in this book.

Step-by-Step

ALL SOUS VIDE COOKING FOLLOWS BASIC STEPS:

1. **SET UP THE EQUIPMENT:** Fill your container with water and insert your circulator. Make

sure the water comes up to the minimum water line on the circulator, plus about an inch to allow for evaporation. Leave about 2 inches of space at the top of the container to allow for displacement of the food when it is added. (If this is not possible, you need a bigger container. Your circulator's instruction manual will tell you the maximum amount of water it can handle.) Make sure that the surface beneath the container can handle the heat. If you're not sure, either use a folded kitchen towel or wooden cutting board to protect the surface or move the vessel to a safer surface. Placing the container on the stovetop is not recommended; it's too easy to accidentally turn on the stove and wreak havoc with the carefully controlled cooking temperature. Not that you would do that. But someone else might.

2. PREHEAT THE WATER: Set your circulator to heat the water to the temperature specified in the recipe. Your sous vide circulator can do this; you can also help it along by heating water on the stovetop or in an electric kettle. (You don't have to nail the target temperature; once you add the water to the container with the sous vide circulator, the circulator will sense the current temperature and gradually adjust it accordingly.

3. SEAL THE FOOD: While the water preheats, set up your food. This means preparing it according to the recipe and sealing it with your preferred method. (See Sealing, page 15.)

4. SUBMERGE AND CHECK THE FOOD: With the water at the correct temperature, place the bag or container in the water. Make sure the water circulates freely around the sealed food, checking to make sure it's not jammed against the side of the container or stuck to the circulator. If the food needs some weight to keep it submerged, place a ramekin or other weight on top of it. (See Weights, page 15.) If you've sealed the food in a zip-top bag, you can also see whether the bag has air bubbles and remove those. (The hot water tends to make the air bubbles more evident.) Don't do this in the sous vide bath; it's hot! (See Sealing, page 15.)

5. COOK: While the water circulates and gurgles, set a timer and handle any preparation necessary for the final touches.

6. FINISH: If you're saving the food for later, skip this step and go straight to Serve or Save, below. Otherwise, know that some foods—many desserts, vegetables, or fish, for example—can be served as is. Others, including most meats, will benefit from a quick sear to develop a crust. Use a paper towel or clean cloth to dry the exterior of the food; a crust forms best when there is no moisture present. (See Finishing, page 18.)

7. SERVE OR SAVE: If you're serving the food now, plate your finished dish. It's ready. If you're saving the food for later, it's time to cool it down. Transfer the package to a bath of half ice, half water until cool (as a general rule, this takes about 20 minutes), and then refrigerate. (See Cooling and Storing Food, page 16.)

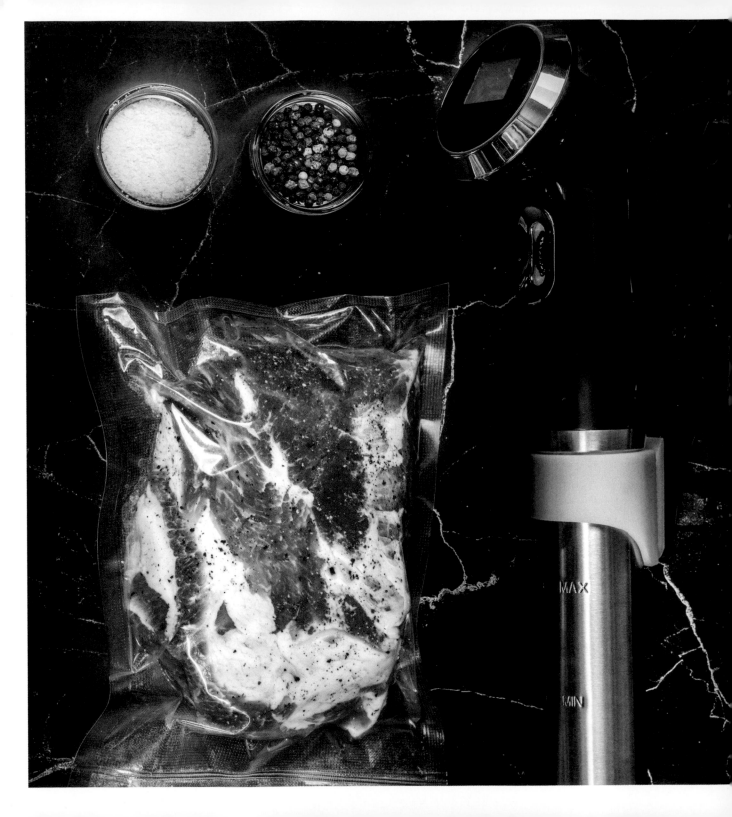

Sous Vide Equipment Recommendations

To cook sous vide, there are only a handful of absolutely necessary pieces of equipment. This is a brief listing of the must-haves, the nice-to-haves, and a few things you really don't need at all and that can actually interfere with the ease of cooking with this method. A more in-depth exploration of each type of equipment follows.

Must-haves

- **SOUS VIDE CIRCULATOR**
- **CONTAINER FOR WATER**

A stockpot will do nicely here—just be sure to take note of the minimum water level for your circulator to function. (I also find it nice when the water jet is submerged; otherwise the flowing water of your sous vide setup may generate a tinkling sound.) Be sure, too, that the water won't overflow when the food is added.

Remember that more water will mean that the temperature will bounce back more quickly when the food is added, which is good. It does mean, though, that the water will take longer to come to temperature in the first place. (You can address this by heating some or all of the water on the stove top. Just make sure that the circulator is not in the vessel if the water is being heated on the stove top when you do this.)

If you use your sous vide setup regularly and have the space, it's worth looking into a purpose-built container. Available online, these containers are typically larger than a pot you might own and have snug-fitting covers with—and this is key—a hole for the sous vide circulator.

Nice to Have

VACUUM SEALER: You can do a lot of sous vide cooking in zip-top freezer bags or canning jars. But if you'd like to expand your kit, a vacuum sealer can be a useful purchase. Not only is it good for preparing food for its sous vide bath, it can also be handy for storing and freezing leftovers and pantry products.

REUSABLE SILICONE BAGS: There's a place for these, although they're not perfect. Because the silicone is thicker and more rigid than plastic, it can be difficult to force the silicone to conform to the shape of the food. This leaves open the possibility of air pockets.

One plus: To clean them, just turn them inside out and run them through the dishwasher.

KITCHEN TORCH: While many of the recipes in this book call for finishing the food in a heavy pan on the stovetop, it's usually possible to use a kitchen torch to achieve the same seared crust. (And in fact, for Sous Vide Crème Brûlée, page 209, it's required.) Is it necessary? It's not. But sometimes it's nice to have an extra tool in the toolbox.

Leave It on the Shelf

PING PONG BALLS: As seen on the internet, these float atop the water and help the water retain heat—in theory. In practice, you will chase them around the kitchen and find one under the dining table two months later. Also, table tennis was not meant to be played at, say, 160°F. In testing, some of mine developed cracks and weird smells. Better to use aluminum foil as a makeshift cover for the cooking vessel or to spend the money on a purpose-built container and cover.

PLASTIC BAGS WITH HAND PUMP: Reusable plastic bags and a hand pump that spares you the expense of a vacuum sealer might seem like an ideal combination of environmental sensitivity and thriftiness. Truly, I wanted to believe. Ultimately, in my experience, these fell short.

The instructions may warn against submerging the seal in the water, forcing you to do a delicate dance—submerged, but not too submerged! I've also found the hand pump fragile.

Sous Vide Circulators

All a circulator really has to do is circulate water and heat it.

That's it. Those requirements don't make up a particularly tall order; there are plenty of machines on the market that tick those two boxes. The tricky part, in my experience, is when companies try to layer features on top of those basic functions. Then you're caught in the position of hoping that their app works, that there's no inconvenient Wi-Fi hiccup, and so on.

WI-FI/BLUETOOTH: Meh. Yes, that's my official recommendation: meh. The feature may allow you to monitor the temperature of the water from another room, but in general there's not much to see here—once the water reaches

temperature, it stays at temperature. The feature may function as a timer, but you probably already have one of those. In general, it's not necessary for cooking and its novelty wore off quickly for me.

WATTAGE: Circulator range typically runs from 800W to 1200W. More wattage means more power to heat the water, but if you're using something along the lines of an 8-quart pot, I've found even the lowest-wattage circulators handily manage to heat the water.

PUMP VOLUME: The rate at which the circulator pumps out water typically ranges from 1.5 gallons to about 3 gallons per minute. More water circulating can mean the temperature is achieved or maintained more readily. Again, unless you're using a very large container, even circulators on the lower end of the range should be adequate.

Containers

There's no magic to choosing a container for the water bath. The size and material can vary, but you probably already have something that will work: A stockpot does the trick. (I most often use an 8-quart pot.) The specific water level necessary will vary by sous vide circulator, but look for the minimum water level line on the circulator and make sure the water reaches an inch or so above that level and does not fall below the line. (Don't overfill the vessel; remember that adding the bagged food will cause the water to rise a bit.)

Restaurant supply stores sell plastic tubs made for food storage and suitable for use as a sous vide vessel. Plastic sous vide containers with custom-made lids are available online. These bins feature a slot for your sous vide circulator, allowing the lid to stay on (and the water to retain heat) while you cook. These are hardly necessary for casual sous vide cooks (they're on the pricier side), but are a worthwhile expenditure if you sous vide frequently. They also allow you to watch the food while it cooks, though I'll be honest: There's not a lot to see here. "A bag sitting in water" neatly summarizes the experience of watching most foods cook sous vide. But there is a tiny bit of theater in getting a window on your food, and clear containers do afford that opportunity.

Consider putting something under the container as well. While the container may not get too hot, it's better to be safe and spare your countertop or work surface from any potential heat damage. A wooden cutting board or a thick kitchen towel should do the trick.

How to Choose and Seal Bags

When it comes to plastic bags, high- and low-density polyethylene (often abbreviated HDPE and LDPE, respectively) and polypropylene bags are acceptable for sous vide. Vinyl chloride polymers are not. Most high-quality zip-top resealable bags, such as Ziploc, are polyethylene.

If you're bagging something that might carry dangerous bacteria, such as chicken, fold back the lip of the bag on itself before placing the chicken in the bag, then unfold and seal the bag. This ensures that any chicken drippings land on the inside of the bag, where you won't touch them.

Zip-Top Bag + Water-Displacement Method

Chances are the manufacturer of your favorite zip-top bag will tell you that they are not intended for sous vide cooking. While that is undoubtedly true, high-quality freezer bags combined with the water-displacement method for chasing the air from the bags (see page 15) are what a lot of people use. Choose quart- or gallon-size bags depending on the amount of food. Make sure they have a double seal, not a sliding-top seal. (A double seal means the top of the bag has two "tracks.")

These bags are not what I prefer (I'm partial to vacuum sealing, see page 15), but I've used them, always with success. One downside is the disposable single-use plastic they entail. My solution to this is to search enthusiastically for other ways to reduce my ecological footprint and to employ reusable silicone bags or glass jars when practical.

Also, be aware that temperatures above about 155°F may cause the seal to fail. For those higher temperatures, stick to silicone bags, vacuum-seal bags, or (if it makes sense) glass jars.

Vacuum Sealer + Storage Bags

Vacuum sealers, such as those made by FoodSaver or Anova, use a roll of food-safe polyethylene plastic for vacuum packing and sealing your food. The roll of plastic allows you to make custom bags to size. (Ready-made bags are also available.) The powerful vacuum makes it easy to remove the air from the bags. One downside: The vacuum can be a little too vigorous, attempting to slurp up any liquids in the bag. The recipes in this book generally use little enough liquid that you can manage, in particular if you tell the machine to seal the bag before it has removed every last trace of air (and liquid). Although the specifics may vary depending on the vacuum sealer, look for a button that says "seal"—that should stop the suction and seal the bag.

These bags also share the ecological downside of plastic zip-top bags. To be more environmentally sensitive, look for manufacturers that offset or reduce their plastic use. Follow the instructions that come with your vacuum sealer in order to use the bags; they're typically quite easy to use.

Reusable Silicone Sous Vide Bag

Reusable bags from companies such as Stasher take advantage of silicone to deliver a food-safe, zip-top alternative to plastic. (If you, like me, did not realize that silicone was not a plastic, what can I say? You're in good company.) Besides being reusable, silicone bags are dishwasher-safe. As with zip-top plastic bags, follow the water-displacement method for chasing the air from the bags (see page 15).

Glass Jars

Sometimes the best "bag" isn't a bag at all: The glass jar in some ways stands as the gold standard for convenience and reusability. While it's not suitable for many recipes (i.e., meat in a glass jar isn't really happening), many of the recipes in the Desserts chapter—such as Silky Lemon Curd (page 197), Berry Cheesecake (page 194), Salted Dulce de Leche (page 204), and more—do call for glass canning jars. Another bonus of using glass jars with canning lids: It's not necessary to get the air out of them before placing them in the sous vide bath. As long as you respect the jar's headspace (the amount of air between the food and the lid) as indicated by the recipe, and tighten the lids properly (tight but not too tight), the water from the sous vide bath will not flow into the jar.

A note about tightening the lids: Most sous vide recipes that use canning jars call for closing the bands "fingertip tight." Fingertip what now? Fingertip tight means securely but not as tight as absolutely possible. So once you find yourself throwing some muscle into it, you've gone too far (unless, of course, those muscles are strictly in your fingertips). The bands need to be tight enough to hold the lids to the jars, but not so tight that the air in the jar can't force itself out. At a loss? The jar experts at Clemson University recommend that you "place the band on the jar, turn it just until you feel resistance, then turn the band one-quarter turn more."

Sealing

WATER DISPLACEMENT: Note that you can either do this in the sink or in the sous vide container itself. I prefer the sink because if some liquid or juice escapes from the bag, it will go down the drain rather than floating in my sous vide bath. But if you do it in the sous vide container, don't wait until the water comes up to temperature; that will probably be uncomfortably hot, possibly even dangerous.

Place the food in a zip-top freezer bag with a double seal or a silicone bag. Seal the bag about halfway and then begin to submerge the bag in water, always keeping the seal above the water line. As the air leaves the bag, the lower part of the bag will sink. When the water comes up just to the zipper of the bag, seal the bag. You should feel the bag click close. Make sure the food is in a single layer, massaging the bag to redistribute the food if necessary.

VACUUM SEALER: Follow the instructions that come with your vacuum sealer in order to use the bags. Generally, cut the roll to size or use a precut bag. Make a cuff on the bag, roll back the cuff, and fill the bag with the food as directed. (Making this double cuff ensures that any raw meat or juices lands on the inside of the bag.) Unfold the cuff, and then seal the bag.

Weights

Meats with air removed from the bag will typically not float; vegetables, on the other hand, will tend to float no matter how diligent you are about removing the air. (Vegetables are notorious offenders here because of the air trapped inside the vegetables themselves.) But you have a solution!

Sous vide weights are available online and work as advertised. It's nice to be able to seal them inside the bag and afterward toss them into the dishwasher. Some models ingeniously include magnets. Arrange them on the outside of the bag and they stay in place by gripping each other through the bag.

Even better—and probably already at hand—is a ramekin or canning jar with no lid, filled with pie weights if handy. (In many cases, the ramekin or jar and the water that fills it will be enough to weigh down the food.) Place it atop the floating bag.

Sous Vide Food Safety

Compared with sous vide cooking, traditional temperature guidelines call for a relatively high internal temperature—for example, cook a chicken breast to 165°F. Those times and temperatures do not address the low temperatures in sous vide cooking.

Start off by choosing products you know are fresh, carefully prepared, and stored according to rigorous safety procedures.

Note that the list on page 16 outlines the amount of time that the food spends at the indicated temperature—food does not instantly come up to temperature when dropped in the water bath! So the actual cooking time needs to be longer than what is shown (thus the "+" symbol).

Times and temperatures for Salmonella destruction		
Temperature (°F)	Time (meat)	Time (poultry)
131°F	89+ minutes	
132°F	71+ minutes	
133°F	56+ minutes	
134°F	45+ minutes	
135°F	36+ minutes	Not safe
136°F	28+ minutes	
137°F	23+ minutes	
138°F	18+ minutes	
139°F	15+ minutes	
140°F	12+ minutes	17+ minutes
141°F	9+ minutes	15.5+ minutes
142°F	8+ minutes	14+ minutes
143°F	6+ minutes	12.5+ minutes
144°F	5+ minutes	11+ minutes
145°F	4+ minutes	9.5+ minutes
146°F	3+ minutes	8+ minutes
147°F	2.5+ minutes	6.5+ minutes
148°F	2+ minutes	5+ minutes
149°F	1.5+ minutes	3.5+ minutes
150°F	1.5+ minutes	2+ minutes
151°F	1+ minutes	1.5+ minutes
152°F	< 1 minute	1.5+ minutes
153°F	< 1 minute	1.5+ minutes
154°F	< 1 minute	1.5+ minutes
155°F	< 1 minute	1+ minute
156°F	< 1 minute	1+ minute
157°F	< 1 minute	1+ minute
158°F	0 minutes	.5+ minute
159°F	0 minutes	< .5 minute

Notes: Some times are rounded up, meaning that in a few cases the actual times required may be a few seconds less, but these temperatures and times err on the side of caution.
Sources: British Columbia Centre for Disease Control, United States Food Safety Inspection Service, American Meat Institute Foundation.
The thickness and shape of food will affect the time required for food to reach the desired temperature. Thinner portions come to temperature faster than thicker portions of the same amount of food.

Temperature Danger Zone

Don't allow food to sit for more than 2 hours between 40°F to 140°F, since those temperatures allow bacteria to reproduce rapidly. Some recipes in this book call for cooking temperatures below 140°F. In those cases, the recipes do not call for cooking longer than 2 hours. Also, food should either be served immediately or rapidly chilled so it spends as little time as possible in that danger zone (see Cooling and Storing Food below).

It's worth noting that the concept of the danger zone is important and useful, but it's a blunt instrument. Food safety means managing risk. The term "danger zone" does of course imply some risk. But many pathogens are killed well below 140°F.

Ultimately, this is a judgment call and, as with eating raw seafood (see opposite), people with compromised immune systems may wish to stay away from those recipes— or bump up the temperature to above 140°F. You'll still have plenty of fun with sous vide.

Cooling and Storing Food

The University of Minnesota and other food safety authorities report that improper cooling is a leading cause of foodborne illness. Food should be served immediately or cooled immediately and stored below 37°F. (Consider purchasing a refrigerator thermometer.) As noted earlier, to cool the food, put it (still in the bag) in a bath of half water and half ice in the refrigerator and bring it below 37°F as quickly as possible. Yes, this takes a lot of ice. Yes, it may be inconvenient. It is still better than food poisoning.

Special Notes on Seafood

Have you seen those warnings on menus about eating raw or undercooked seafood? There's a warning like that for sous vide seafood, too: The seafood temperatures in this book do not result in pasteurization and thus do not destroy bacteria and reduce risk. You should not cook any seafood sous vide that you would not be happy to eat raw. No matter what the finished product may look like—perhaps charred on the outside and pleasingly pink in the center—the seafood has not been cooked at a pathogen-destroying temperature. It may look cosmetically cooked, but it is for most intents and purposes raw seafood.

I eat raw seafood. You may eat raw seafood, too. Or you may not! There are reasonable cases on both sides. But everyone should know what they're eating and that's why I want to be very clear: For food-safety purposes, eating seafood cooked sous vide is the same as eating raw seafood. Consuming raw or undercooked seafood may increase your risk of foodborne illness, especially if you have certain medical conditions.

Freezing seafood may be necessary to reduce or eliminate parasites. (Yes, I know: Yum!) Purchasing frozen seafood neatly takes care of this. You may also freeze the seafood at home for seven days before cooking it to ensure that parasites are killed.

Cooking from Frozen

Cooking from frozen is possible and easy with sous vide, but should be avoided with large hunks of meat, since the cores of that meat may linger near dangerous temperatures for too long. Generally, steaks, cutlets, and ribs are fine. Something like a whole pork shoulder would present a risk. The solution for something like the Carnitas-Style Pork Shoulder (page 53) is to freeze it in the required 2-inch cubes.

Here's the general rule: Cook frozen meats at the same temperature as indicated in the recipe, but for 50% more time. So, for example, 1 hour 30 minutes (90 minutes) turns into 2 hours 15 minutes (90 minutes × 1.5 = 135 minutes). This rule of thumb allows plenty of time for the food to thaw, while taking advantage of the built-in "fudge factor" of sous vide cooking (i.e., most foods can be cooked sous vide for longer than the prescribed time without being overcooked).

Finishing

Because food emerges from the sous vide bath cooked but not browned, most meat and poultry recipes call for finishing the food with high heat. This allows the meat or poultry to develop a nice crust, providing not only aesthetic appeal but texture and taste as well. (Most egg and vegetable recipes—and some fish and seafood recipes—don't require finishing.)

THERE ARE A FEW WAYS TO FINISH YOUR FOOD:

ON THE STOVETOP: Most recipes call for finishing the food on the stovetop. This is the most straightforward method. You're looking to provide a lot of heat in a little time, which is why a heavy pan (cast iron, for example) is recommended. In many cases, the high heat will generate smoke. This is a good time to switch on your exhaust fan. If you want to make grill marks on the stovetop, look for a stovetop grill pan (often cast iron).

UNDER THE BROILER: Some of the dishes in this book, such as Simply Salt and Pepper Pork Ribs (page 71), call for finishing under the broiler. The broiler provides a lot of heat quickly, which is what we're looking for. On the other hand, it can also be unforgiving and lead quickly to burnt food. The proximity of the heating element to the food (sometimes as little as a few inches) and the recommended broiling times (perhaps 1 or 2 minutes) don't leave wide margins for error. Check your broiled food early and often.

WITH A TORCH: While only one dish in this book, Sous Vide Crème Brûlée (page 209), calls for a torch, you may reach for it for other dishes (and if you received your sous vide circulator as a gift, there's a chance you unwrapped a torch, too). Most of the dishes that call for finishing on the stovetop can instead be finished with a torch. Take care to read the safety instructions that come with the torch and respect that you are literally playing with fire. Start with the flame far away from the food and draw it closer gradually to avoid scorching the food. Move the torch slowly and evenly across the food, adjusting the flame if the surface is browning too quickly or too slowly.

ON THE BARBECUE: Because cast-iron pans can go on the grill, one option is to treat your barbecue as a stovetop and finish the food in a cast-iron pan on the grill. Or you can place the food directly on the grill. Brush the clean grill grates with vegetable oil. (If you don't have a brush, use tongs to wield a paper towel dipped in oil.) Preheat one side of the grill to high heat. When the grates are very hot, reduce the heat to low and place the food on the hot grates until it picks up grill marks, about 1 minute (possibly less). While it grills, use a spatula to gently press down on the food to ensure contact with the grates. Flip and repeat on the other side.

Remember that you're not trying to cook the food, you're just looking for a nice finish. Leaving the food on the grill too long can lead to overcooked food.

FAQ

How do you pronounce sous vide?

It's French for "under vacuum," and if you're speaking to other English-speakers, something along the lines of "sue veed" gets the job done.

Which recipe should I start with?

To get a feel for sous vide setup and equipment, start with something simple: Perfectly Poached Eggs (page 156) are already in a container (their shell). Then move on to the unpretentious stars of the sous vide scene: either Simple Sous Vide Skirt Steak (page 79) or The Perfect Pork Chops (page 47).

When I add the food to the water bath, the temperature drops. Is that okay?

Yes. Don't wait for the water to come back to temperature before starting the timer. The drop of a few degrees at the start of cooking is already accounted for in the recipe. (It probably won't take more than a few minutes for the water to come back to temperature, and meanwhile the food is approaching the target temperature.)

Help! The bag is floating. What do I do?

Hot water has a way of discovering hidden air, whether it's in the bag or (just as likely) within the food itself (vegetables, especially). There are a few ways to work against this: Drop either a ramekin or a canning jar into the water bath on top of the bag. It will weigh down the food and keep it submerged. If this doesn't work or you don't have a ramekin, insert a weight or two into the bag (see Weights, page 15).

The water bath is splashing all over the counter and I'm afraid the water level will get too low.

It's a simple fix: Just make a "lid" from a piece of aluminum foil to lightly cover the pot.

If I chill the meat before finishing it, how do I make sure it's warmed throughout when serving it?

Simply taking the refrigerator-cold meat and popping it under the broiler or on the stovetop may not warm the meat all the way through. The best way to solve that problem is to sous vide the meat for about 15 minutes at the original cooking temperature and then finish it.

What about sous vide cooking at altitude?

We know that altitude affects the boiling point of water. But the good news is that because sous vide cooking takes place well below the boiling point, the temperature for sous vide cooking is unaffected by altitude. There is one possible difference that bears mentioning: The water may evaporate out of the bath more quickly than at sea level. This is easily managed by starting with more water and occasionally refilling if necessary.

How do I clean my sous vide circulator?

Your sous vide circulator may accumulate minerals from the water, especially on the heating element. To remove the mineral accumulation, wipe the plastic exterior with a damp cloth. To clean the heating element: Combine equal parts water and distilled white vinegar in the smallest vessel possible for your circulator. Set the circulator to 140°F. Once it reaches temperature, turn off the circulator, carefully pour the vinegar and water out, and then dip or rinse the circulator in water. You may also put a few tablespoons of white vinegar in the water bath to regularly clean the machine.

What's the right amount of water in the container?

There's no single answer, but it's easy to figure out: You need enough water to completely immerse the food being cooked, enough to come up to the minimum level for the sous vide circulator (sometimes marked on the device, sometimes signaled with an error message when it's too low), but not so much that the circulator can't keep up with heating the water. Your circulator's manual will say how much water it can handle.

How long does the water take to reach temperature?

This depends on the amount of water and its starting temperature, whether the container is covered, the brand of sous vide circulator, and the target temperature. These figures are guidelines based on cold tap water and an 8-quart pot. Note that it's better to start heating the water earlier, since the water can stay at temperature for as long as you'd like:

115-129°F: 25 minutes
130-150°F: 40 minutes
151-175°F: 1 hour
176-185°F: 1 hour 30 minutes

To give things a head start, give your circulator an assist: Heat some water on the stovetop or in an electric kettle and use that water to fill your sous vide container. There's no need to get the temperature exactly right. The sous vide circulator will detect the water's temperature and heat it up further or allow it to cool—if necessary.

What can I do with the water in the bath when I'm done with it?

As long as the container with the food hasn't leaked, the water is fine to reuse for another sous vide project. Once it's cooled, you may also choose to use it to water the plants or give to the dog. (Actually, the dog would probably love it if the bag had leaked, but that's another story.)

Should the container be cleaned after each use?

If you know you'll be cooking sous vide again soon, there's no need to clean it unless the bag has leaked. If you plan to use the container for other things—if we're talking about your soup vat or spaghetti pot—then give it a quick wipe-down and rinse. Depending on the hardness of your water, minerals may accumulate, and it can be nice to keep things tidy.

Why no raw garlic in these recipes?

In short, garlic that goes in raw would come out raw. The sous vide temperatures that cook meat are not sufficient to cook garlic. For this reason, some recipes here use garlic powder. Another option: Cook the garlic on the stove beforehand while pre-searing the meat. (Simple Sous Vide Duck Breasts, page 111, take this route.)

Can I double the recipes? What about big-batch cooking?

As long as there is space in your sous vide bath, sure. One caution: Use separate bags (or jars) for the extra food—do not overstuff the bags or use larger jars, as this may affect the cooking time. Just as the recipes can be doubled, they can accommodate big-batch cooking (e.g., for a barbecue). The caveat is to make sure the food does not spend too much time in temperature danger zone (see Food Safety, page 15). Either finish and serve the food immediately after sous vide cooking or safely cool it and finish just before serving (see Cooling and Storing Food, page 16).

Can I swap out the table salt in these recipes for a fancy or chunky salt?

In general, you can use other types of salt as long as you substitute an equivalent quantity. Note that 1 teaspoon of table salt is not the same as 1 teaspoon of kosher salt. The grains of kosher salt are larger and so are not packed as densely in the spoon. In short, you need more kosher salt by volume (so, by the teaspoon, for example) to reach the equivalent amount of table salt. To add to the confusion, even different brands of kosher salt measure differently by volume! Fine sea salt can sometimes be swapped out in equal measure, but, of course, it depends on the sea salt.

Using These Recipes

I try to approach cooking strategically and I want to help you do that, too. So let me explain how this book is arranged:

Basic recipes—such as Simple Sous Vide Chicken Breasts (page 26)—are labeled as such, so if you want to begin by mastering the method with something straightforward, you know where to start. Many of these foundational recipes are followed by practical and delicious ways to incorporate them into mealtime. Look for the red "Make It a Meal and More" labels, such as those on pages 27, 29, and 30, which offer more elaborate uses for the Simple Sous Vide Chicken Breasts.

Other recipes present a tasty but straightforward version and then a simple, delicious twist. (For example, The Perfect Pork Tenderloin, page 56, is followed by a peanut-sesame variation.)

"Surprisingly Sous Vide" sections showcase unexpected applications for the sous vide technique, such as Shortcut "Cold Brew" Coffee (page 212) and Pasteurized Eggs (page 167). Think of them as the answer to "Yeah, but besides meat, what else can sous vide do?" You'll find these sprinkled throughout the book.

CHAPTER 2

Chicken & Turkey

Even if I'm going to use chicken breasts right away, I find the small amount of work it takes to sous vide them has a few advantages: perfectly cooked chicken, minimal fiddling with raw chicken, and no prodding or guessing to determine whether the chicken is fully cooked. And of course, sous vide cooking can go way beyond chicken breasts. Moist, flavorful thighs; tender golden brown drumsticks; and even a turkey breast show off what the sous vide technique can do.

Simple Sous Vide Chicken Breasts

TOTAL TIME: 1 hour 40 minutes   **ACTIVE TIME:** 10 minutes   **YIELD:** Serves 4

Something so perfectly simple as a chicken breast is not just a meal in its own right—although of course it can be—but, as you'll see in the following pages, can be spun into any number of meals. Consider sous-viding some chicken breasts as a huge down payment on a delicious meal down the line.

---

4 boneless, skinless chicken breasts (about 2½ pounds)

1 teaspoon table salt

1 teaspoon freshly ground black pepper

2 tablespoons neutral-flavored vegetable oil, such as corn or canola

---

1 Set the water temperature to 150°F. Season the chicken evenly on both sides with salt and pepper. Place the chicken in the bag and pour in 1 tablespoon of the oil. Seal the bag.

2 When the water reaches temperature, place the bagged chicken in the water. After 1 hour 30 minutes, remove the bagged chicken from the water. (If you're refrigerating the chicken, chill it first in a bath of half water and half ice until cold, about 30 minutes, before refrigerating.)

3 To brown the chicken: Remove the chicken from the bag and discard the juices. Pat the chicken dry with paper towels. Heat the remaining vegetable oil in a large skillet over medium-high heat, until shimmering, about

1 minute. Working in batches, if necessary, gently place the chicken breasts in the pan and sear each side until browned, about 1 minute 30 seconds per side. Transfer to a plate and cover with aluminum foil until ready to serve.

Simple Sous Vide Chicken Breasts will keep, in an airtight container in the refrigerator, for up to 3 days.

Lemon-Za'atar Chicken Breasts

In Step 1, add the juice of 3 medium lemons (about 8 tablespoons) and 3 tablespoons za'atar to the bag with the chicken. In Step 3, there's no need to dry the chicken—the sugars in the lemon juice will caramelize for a nice crust.

3 IDEAS FOR SIMPLE SOUS VIDE CHICKEN BREASTS: SERVED WARM

Chicken with Butter and Scallions

Prep Note: You'll need 4 Simple Sous Vide Chicken Breasts (page 26) prepared through Step 2.

Melt 4 tablespoons unsalted butter in a skillet over medium-low heat. Add 6 thick or 12 thin scallions, thinly sliced and dark green ends discarded. Cook until the scallions are very soft and almost saucy, about 15 minutes. (Turn down the heat if the scallions start to brown.)

Add the Simple Chicken Breasts, cut into bite-size pieces. Turn off the heat. Let the scallions cool until just warm, about 5 minutes. Stir in 2 large beaten pasteurized egg yolks; 1 large handful flat-leaf parsley, finely chopped; ½ cup freshly grated Parmesan cheese; and a generous grind of black pepper. Serves 4.

Chicken with Cavatappi and Basil Pesto

Prep Note: You'll need 2 Simple Sous Vide Chicken Breasts (page 26) prepared through Step 2.

In a food processor, pulse 1 very large bunch of basil (large stems removed), 1 palm-sized hunk of Parmesan (broken into chunks), 1 generous glug of extra-virgin olive oil, and a pinch of table salt. Adjust ingredients to taste.

In a large pot, cook 1 pound cavatappi pasta according to package directions, tasting a piece of pasta 2 minutes short of the minimum recommended cooking time and every 30 seconds thereafter. When the pasta has a firm bite (it will still cook a bit more), remove and drain, reserving about 1 cup cooking water.

Place the drained pasta back in the pot with about ½ cup of pasta water, all of the pesto, and the Simple Chicken Breasts, cut into bite-size pieces. Stir gently until the sauce is evenly distributed and creamy, adding more pasta water if necessary. Serves 4.

Chicken with Coconut Jasmine Rice

Prep Note: You'll need 4 Simple Chicken Breasts (page 26) prepared through Step 2.

Rinse 2 cups jasmine rice in a fine-mesh sieve several times until the water runs clear. Drain the excess water. Place the rice in a medium-size pot and add 1 can (13½ ounces) coconut milk, 1½ cups water, 1 teaspoon table salt, and 1 teaspoon sugar. Bring the mixture to a boil over high heat. Turn the heat to low and cook, covered, for 20 minutes.

Reheat the Simple Chicken Breasts in the microwave (without the bags) or by placing the bagged chicken in 140°F sous vide bath for about 10 minutes.

Uncover the rice and cook for 5 minutes more. Fluff and divide the rice among 4 plates. Slice each chicken breast and fan out one breast atop each pile of rice. Garnish with chopped cilantro and serve hot. Serves 4.

Chicken with Snow Peas and Carrots (page 29)

MORE IDEAS FOR SIMPLE
SOUS VIDE CHICKEN BREASTS: SERVED WARM

Chicken with Snow Peas and Carrots

Prep Note: You'll need 2 Simple Sous Vide Chicken Breasts (page 26) prepared through Step 2.

In a small bowl, mix ¼ cup fresh lime juice, 2 tablespoons soy sauce, 1 tablespoon brown sugar, 1 teaspoon cornstarch, ½ teaspoon freshly ground black pepper, and ¼ teaspoon red pepper flakes. Heat a large skillet or wok over high heat. When a drop of water vaporizes in 1 to 2 seconds, add 1 tablespoon vegetable oil and swirl to coat. Add 3 cups carrots sliced ½ inch thick. Stir-fry for 2 minutes. Swirl in another 1 tablespoon vegetable oil, then add 2 cloves garlic, finely chopped, and 3 cups trimmed snow peas (these are the thin, flat peas with edible pods). Stir-fry until the vegetables are tender, about 3 minutes more. Place the Simple Chicken Breasts, cut into bite-size pieces, in the skillet. Add the reserved sauce and cook, gently stirring, until well coated and hot, about 1 minute. Serve with rice. Serves 4.

Shake-ish and Bake-ish

Prep Note: You'll need 4 Simple Sous Vide Chicken Breasts (page 26) prepared through Step 2.

In a shallow bowl, mix 1 cup unseasoned breadcrumbs, 2 teaspoons onion powder, 2 teaspoons dried parsley, 2 teaspoons dried basil, 1 teaspoon table salt, 1 teaspoon paprika, 1 teaspoon garlic powder, 1 teaspoon sugar, and ½ teaspoon freshly ground black pepper. In a second shallow bowl, mix together 1 large beaten egg and 1 tablespoon milk. Working with one at a time, dip the Simple Chicken Breasts into the egg mixture and shake off the excess. Place each chicken breast in the coating mixture, pressing to coat well, and set aside on a platter until you're ready to cook. Heat 2 tablespoons neutral-flavored vegetable oil in a large skillet over medium-high heat. When the oil is shimmering, about 2 minutes, place two chicken breasts in the skillet and cook until golden brown and crispy, about 2 minutes on each side. Place the chicken breasts on a plate, cover with aluminum foil, and repeat with the last two chicken breasts in the same oil. Serve hot. Serves 4.

4 IDEAS FOR SIMPLE
SOUS VIDE CHICKEN BREASTS: SERVED CHILLED

Chicken with Romaine, Feta, and Salad Crunch

Prep Note: You'll need 2 Simple Sous Vide Chicken Breasts (page 26) prepared through Step 3.

In a very large bowl (salads are better tossed with ample space), place the torn leaves of 1 large washed head of romaine lettuce and 6 ounces of crumbled feta cheese. Place ¼ cup shelled unsalted sunflower seeds and ¼ cup unsalted pumpkin seeds in a large dry skillet over medium heat. Cook, shaking the pan often, until gently toasted and fragrant, about 4 minutes. Pour the seeds on the salad, then add ½ cup dried cranberries and toss. Add the Simple Chicken Breasts, cut into bite-size pieces, and toss. Dress with a generous squeeze of fresh lemon juice and extra-virgin olive oil, and then toss again. Serves 4.

Chicken with Chilled Sesame Soba Noodles

Prep Note: You'll need 3 Simple Sous Vide Chicken Breasts (page 26) prepared through Step 2 and chilled.

Cook 8 ounces soba noodles according to the package directions. Rinse under cold water and drain. Set the noodles aside. In a small bowl, whisk together ¼ cup rice vinegar, 2 tablespoons soy sauce, 1 tablespoon toasted sesame oil, 1 tablespoon sugar, 1 clove garlic, minced, and 1 teaspoon grated ginger. In a large bowl, combine the noodles, rice vinegar dressing, and the Simple Chicken Breasts, cut into bite-size pieces. Garnish with sesame seeds and finely chopped scallions. Serves 4.

Chicken Salad with Mixed Beans and Avocado

Prep Note: You'll need 2 Simple Sous Vide Chicken Breasts (page 26) prepared through Step 2 and chilled.

In a colander, drain 1 can (15 ounces) of garbanzo beans and 1 can (15 ounces) of black beans. Rinse the beans well and shake the water off the beans in the colander. Add the Simple Sous Vide Chicken Breasts, cut into bite-size pieces, to the beans and mix well. Add ½ cup jarred reduced-sodium salsa and stir into the salad, tasting and adding more salsa if desired. Add ½ cup crushed tortilla chips and gently stir. Gently stir 1 avocado, diced, into the salad. Dress with the juice of 1 fresh lime and a generous glug of extra-virgin olive oil, then gently toss again. Serves 4.

Chicken Sandwiches with Havarti and Mustard

Prep Note: You'll need 2 Simple Sous Vide Chicken Breasts (page 26) prepared through Step 2 and chilled.

Evenly spread 8 slices of whole wheat or hearty white bread with Dijon mustard and place a slice of Havarti cheese over 4 of the bread slices. Halve the Simple Chicken Breasts lengthwise. Place each half on the cheese-topped bread slices. Slice 2 Granny Smith apples about ¼ inch thick and pile the slices on top of the chicken. Top with remaining bread slices. Serves 4.

Chicken Breasts with Preserved Lemon

TOTAL TIME: 1 hour 40 minutes   **ACTIVE TIME:** 10 minutes   **YIELD:** Serves 4

If you haven't used preserved lemons before, here's your introduction: Preserved lemons are one of those almost sneaky "power ingredients" that can sit unassumingly in the fridge for months and then spring into action when called upon to improve mealtime. (They are charmed to meet you, I'm sure.) They are often rinsed before using and sometimes only the rind is used, but in this recipe, we keep both the flesh and the salt for simplicity and flavor.

4 boneless, skinless chicken breasts (about 2½ pounds)

2 tablespoons extra-virgin olive oil

1 small preserved lemon (about 4 ounces), finely chopped, seeds discarded (see box, page 32)

1 teaspoon freshly ground black pepper

Fresh lemon, very thinly sliced, for garnish

1 Set the water temperature to 150°F. Place the chicken, olive oil, preserved lemon, and pepper in the bag and then seal the bag. Massage the bag gently to distribute the lemon and pepper.

2 When the water reaches temperature, place the bagged chicken in the water. After 1 hour 30 minutes, remove the chicken. Pour the chicken and juices into a large skillet over medium-high heat.

Cook, using a spatula to scrape up any stuck lemon bits, until the juices have been slightly reduced, about 2 minutes.

3 Using tongs, transfer the chicken to a platter and pour the juices over. Garnish with the lemon slices and serve hot.

Chicken Breasts with Preserved Lemon will keep, in an airtight container in the refrigerator, for up to 3 days.

PRESERVED LEMONS

Preserved lemons are lemons that have been immersed in salt until the salinity permeates their flesh. They are often available at stores that stock Middle Eastern products, will last practically forever in the refrigerator, and—besides being the cornerstone of this recipe—are an easy way to add zip to a pasta dish or salad. A little goes a long way, so start small and ramp up if desired.

If you'd like to make your own, it's easy and requires three ingredients: lemon, salt, and time.

Scrub about 6 lemons, enough to fit tightly in a medium-size jar with a secure lid. (Have a few more lemons on hand in case they're needed.) Cut each lemon from the top to within about ½ inch of the bottom, cutting the fruit almost into quarters while keeping the sections connected at bottom. Rub kosher salt over the cut surfaces, then put the lemon back together. (It doesn't have to look like it just came off the tree; you're not going to fool anyone here.) Cover the bottom of the jar with kosher salt. Fit all the lemons inside the jar, sprinkling salt on each layer. (It's okay to break them apart. Just make sure they're tightly packed.)

Press the lemons down to release their juices and then squeeze additional lemons into the jar if necessary, until all lemons are immersed in juice.

Close the jar and let it stand at room temperature, shaking the jar every day, for 3 weeks. When the rinds are tender, the lemons are ready to store in the refrigerator.

To use, remove a piece of lemon and rinse it, discarding the seeds and pulp if preferred or if indicated by the recipe.

Chicken Breasts à la Keema Biryani

TOTAL TIME: 1 hour 40 minutes   **ACTIVE TIME:** 10 minutes   **YIELD:** Serves 4

Sometimes I can't say exactly how a recipe comes to be, but in this case I can: This dish owes its origins to a podcast episode (thanks, *Spilled Milk!*) that pointed me to a blog post by cookbook author Ashley Singh Thomas. The recipe lives on her site, My Heart Beets, as "Instant Pot Keema Biryani (Spiced Ground Meat and Rice)," but I rejiggered it to reflect the same flavors in this dish. (Side note: I've made the original dish, too, and it was delicious.)

---

4 boneless, skinless chicken breasts (about 2½ pounds)

3 tablespoons extra-virgin olive oil

1 tablespoon ground coriander

2 teaspoons sweet paprika (see Note)

1 teaspoon table salt

1 teaspoon freshly ground black pepper

1 teaspoon garam masala

1 teaspoon turmeric

¼ teaspoon cayenne pepper

1 tablespoon neutral flavored vegetable oil, such as corn or canola

Cilantro, for garnish

Rice, for serving

---

1 Set the water temperature to 150°F. Place the chicken, olive oil, coriander, paprika, salt, black pepper, garam masala, turmeric, and cayenne pepper in the bag and then seal the bag. Massage the bag gently to distribute the spices throughout the bag. When the water reaches temperature, place the bagged chicken in the water.

2 After 1 hour 30 minutes, remove the bagged chicken. Remove the chicken from the bag, reserving the juices. (See Tip for how to use the juices to make rice.) Pat the chicken dry with paper towels.

3 Heat the vegetable oil in a large skillet over medium-high heat until shimmering, about 1 minute. Working in batches if necessary, gently place the chicken breasts in the pan and sear until browned, about 1 minute 30 seconds each side. Transfer to a serving platter and cover with foil to keep

warm. Garnish with the cilantro and serve hot with rice.

Chicken Breasts à la Keema Biryani will keep, in an airtight container in the refrigerator, for up to 3 days.

NOTE Paprika encompasses varieties that are mild to spicy, with some including smoky notes. "Sweet" paprika is often labeled simply "paprika" and typically does not have smoky notes and does not have much if any heat. That's what you're looking for here, although smoky varieties (often labeled "Spanish paprika") can be used. If you use a spicy variety, consider reducing or eliminating the recipe's cayenne pepper.

TIP
The reserved drippings will last 3 days in a covered container in the refrigerator, or 3 months in a zip-top bag in the freezer. To use the drippings to cook rice, substitute 1½ cups of water with 1¼ cups of water and ¼ cup of drippings. Be advised: They're spicy!

Butter Chicken Thighs

TOTAL TIME: 1 hour 45 minutes   **ACTIVE TIME:** 15 minutes   **YIELD:** Serves 3

Sometime during the Instant Pot fever of the 2010s, Urvashi Pitre, the "Butter Chicken Lady," rose to prominence. She was even in the *New Yorker*! It was hard to escape her butter chicken. Not that you'd want to. It's delicious. Here, I used her famous recipe as a starting point and adapted it to take advantage of the perfect temperature control of sous vide cooking.

1 teaspoon garam masala

½ teaspoon garlic powder

½ teaspoon turmeric

½ teaspoon smoked (or Spanish) paprika

½ teaspoon ground cumin

½ teaspoon table salt

¼ teaspoon cayenne pepper

¼ teaspoon ground ginger

1 pound boneless, skinless chicken thighs

4 tablespoons (½ stick) unsalted butter, cut into small cubes

4 tablespoons heavy cream

¼ cup chopped cilantro

2 tablespoons tomato paste

Rice, for serving

1 Set the water temperature to 165°F. In a small bowl, mix ½ teaspoon garam masala, the garlic powder, turmeric, paprika, cumin, salt, cayenne pepper, and ginger. Dust the chicken evenly with the spice mixture. Pour any remaining spices into the bag.

2 Place the chicken in the bag and evenly distribute 2 tablespoons of the butter. Seal the bag.

3 When the water reaches temperature, place the bagged chicken in the water. After 1 hour 30 minutes, remove the bagged chicken. Remove the chicken from the bag and set it aside.

4 Pour the juices from the bag into a blender. Add 2 tablespoons cream, the cilantro, the remaining ½ teaspoon of garam masala, and the tomato paste. Blend until smooth, about 10 seconds. (Take care when blending hot liquids to leave open the vent on the blender lid.)

5 Pour the blended sauce into a medium-size skillet over medium heat. Add the remaining 2 tablespoons of butter and the remaining 2 tablespoons of cream. Cook, stirring gently, until the butter is melted and the sauce becomes homogenous, about 1 minute.

6 Gently place the chicken in the pan and stir to coat. Cook over medium-low heat, about 1 minute. Divide the chicken and sauce among plates and serve hot with rice.

Butter Chicken Thighs will keep, in an airtight container in the refrigerator, for up to 3 days.

TIP

Save the sauce! Any extra sauce can be refrigerated in a covered glass container for up to 5 days. Serve over rice, roasted vegetables, or, of course, chicken.

Sesame-Chile Chicken Thighs

TOTAL TIME: 1 hour 45 minutes **ACTIVE TIME:** 15 minutes **YIELD:** Serves 3

Even white-meat partisans may be swayed by the rich flavor and texture of these chicken thighs. Pleasingly sweet and more mouth-tingly than outright spicy, they really fire on all cylinders. Of course, for a spicier kick, you can increase the cayenne pepper. (Don't go too far the first time through; a little goes a long way.) Serve with a simple side salad—perhaps with more sesame oil as dressing—along with a bed of plain white rice to perfectly complement the main attraction.

2 tablespoons dark brown sugar

¾ teaspoon table salt

¼ teaspoon garlic powder

½ teaspoon ground ginger

¼ teaspoon allspice

Pinch of cayenne pepper

Pinch of red pepper flakes

Zest of 1 small orange

1 pound boneless, skinless chicken thighs

2 tablespoons toasted sesame oil

⅓ cup untoasted black and/or white sesame seeds

Rice, for serving

Cilantro, large stems removed, for garnish

1 Set the water temperature to 165°F. In a small bowl, mix the brown sugar, salt, garlic powder, ginger, allspice, cayenne pepper, pepper flakes, and orange zest. Sprinkle the chicken evenly with the spice mixture.

2 Place the chicken in the bag, then pour in the sesame oil. Seal the bag and massage it to evenly distribute the spices and oil and to ensure the chicken is in a single layer.

When the water reaches temperature, place the bagged chicken in the water.

3 After 1 hour 25 minutes, prepare the sesame seeds: In a large nonstick pan over medium heat, toast the seeds, shaking the pan often, until fragrant and just starting to turn golden brown, about 5 minutes.

4 After 1 hour 30 minutes total, remove the bagged chicken from the water. Remove the chicken from the bag and place it in the skillet with the toasted sesame seeds. Reserve half of the liquid in the bag.

5 Cook the seeds and the chicken over medium-low heat for 1 minute, using a spatula to gently toss the chicken and coat it in sesame seeds. Once the chicken is coated, add the reserved liquid from the bag to the pan and stir gently to distribute (see Note).

6 Serve the chicken hot, drizzled with sesame seeds and juices from the pan, over a bed of rice. Garnish with cilantro.

Sesame-Chile Chicken Thighs will keep, in an airtight container in the refrigerator, for up to 3 days.

NOTE There's no need to measure the juices to determine what half is; you can eyeball it. Just know that the dish will likely be too salty if you add all of the juices.

GB&D Drumsticks

TOTAL TIME: 1 hour 50 minutes   **ACTIVE TIME:** 15 minutes   **YIELD:** 6 drumsticks

The restaurant world has coined a three-letter expression that means everything: GB&D (golden brown and delicious). Here, the sous vide poaching makes sure the meat is done to perfection and the flavor is distributed throughout. Cooking them sous vide combines the tenderness of slow, gentle cooking with the beautiful golden brown of a broiler finish. After a short stint in a hot oven, these poached and broiled drumsticks are G, B, and definitely D.

¼ cup finely chopped scallions (green and white parts), plus extra green parts, minced, for garnish

¼ cup soy sauce

¼ cup water

2 tablespoons dark brown sugar

1 tablespoon rice vinegar

½ teaspoon ground ginger

½ teaspoon garlic powder

Pinch of cayenne pepper

6 chicken drumsticks (about 1½ pounds)

1 Set the water temperature to 155°F. In a small bowl, whisk the chopped scallions, soy sauce, water, brown sugar, rice vinegar, ground ginger, garlic powder, and cayenne pepper.

2 Pour the liquid into a bag and place the drumsticks in the bag. Seal the bag. Massage it gently to evenly distribute the spices and to ensure the chicken is in a single layer. When the water reaches temperature, place the bagged chicken in the water.

3 After 1 hour, preheat the oven to 500°F.

4 After 1 hour 30 minutes total, remove the bagged chicken from the water bath. Remove the drumsticks from the bag and place them on a rack in a roasting pan. Discard the liquid.

5 Place the chicken in the oven and cook until the chicken is dark brown, about 15 minutes. Garnish with the minced scallions and serve hot.

Sous Vide GB&D Drumsticks will keep, in an airtight container in the refrigerator, for up to 3 days.

Turkey Breast with Poppy-Sesame Greens

TOTAL TIME: 2 hours 50 minutes   **ACTIVE TIME:** 20 minutes   **YIELD:** Serves 4

Poppy and sesame seeds bring a little crunch to quickly cooked greens, while the turkey breast comes out perfectly succulent thanks to no-fuss sous vide cooking.

1½ pounds boneless, skinless turkey breast

1½ teaspoons table salt, plus extra for the greens

1 teaspoon freshly ground black pepper

3 tablespoons extra-virgin olive oil

2 tablespoons poppy seeds

2 tablespoons untoasted sesame seeds

2 large bunches cooking greens, large leaves chopped and large stems removed, about 12 packed cups (see Note)

2 medium cloves garlic, thinly sliced

1 small pinch of ground nutmeg

1 lemon, cut into wedges

Crushed red pepper flakes, for serving

---

1 Set the water temperature to 150°F. Season the turkey evenly on both sides with salt and pepper. Place the turkey breast in the bag and pour in 1 tablespoon of the extra-virgin olive oil. Seal the bag.

2 When the water reaches temperature, place the bagged turkey in the water.

3 After 2 hours 20 minutes (about 10 minutes before the turkey is done), toast the seeds: In a small skillet, toast the poppy and sesame seeds over medium heat, shaking the skillet occasionally, until the poppy seeds begin to pop and the

sesame seeds turn golden, about 5 minutes. Remove the skillet from the heat.

4 After 2 hours 30 minutes, remove the bagged turkey from the water bath. Remove the turkey from the bag, place it on a cutting board, and cover it tightly with aluminum foil.

5 Pour ¼ cup of the juices from the bag into a ramekin. (If there aren't enough juices to make ¼ cup, add enough reduced-sodium chicken broth or water to make ¼ cup.)

6 Prepare the greens: In a large skillet with a lid, heat the remaining 2 tablespoons olive oil over medium heat. Add the garlic. When the garlic begins to sizzle, about 2 minutes, add the greens and turkey juices, tossing to coat. (It's okay if the greens barely fit in the skillet at first; they will cook down a *lot*.)

7 Cook the greens, covered, until they begin to wilt, about 2 minutes. Stir the greens, re-cover, and continue to cook until the greens are very wilted. Uncover and cook the greens until most of the liquid has evaporated, about 2 minutes. Stir in the nutmeg, toasted seeds, and a pinch of salt. Squeeze a lemon wedge over the greens.

8 Place the greens on a warmed serving platter. Cut the breast into ¼- to ½-inch slices and fan slices out over the greens. Serve hot with lemon wedges and a sprinkling of crushed red pepper, if you wish.

Turkey Breast with Poppy-Sesame Greens will keep, in an airtight container in the refrigerator, for up to 3 days.

NOTE Cooking greens include spinach, beet greens, chard, and kale, and any combination will work well here.

CHAPTER 3

Pork

Few things go from fantastic to tragic so easily as a good piece of pork improperly cooked. Using the sous vide cooking method, there's no guesswork involved and no dry, rubbery meat on the table. In this chapter, perfect pork chops await, along with faultless tenderloin, fall-apart juicy carnitas style pork shoulder, and intensely tasty ribs.

The Perfect Pork Chops

TOTAL TIME: 1 hour 40 minutes   **ACTIVE TIME:** 10 minutes   **YIELD:** Serves 4

Overcooked pork chops are dry, chewy, and sad. Perfectly cooked sous vide pork chops, on the other hand, offer a shining example of what's possible with precision cooking—juicy, tender, and meaty at a perfect medium-rare. (Also, shout-out to the saffron and raisin variation, where the saffron imbues the pork with a subtle, well-paired richness and the raisins provide little sweet, porky bursts.)

---

4 bone-in pork chops, ¾ inch thick
    (about 2 pounds)

1 teaspoon table salt

½ teaspoon freshly ground black pepper, plus
    more for finishing

Coarse salt, such as kosher or sea salt,
    for finishing

1 tablespoon neutral-flavored vegetable oil, such
    as corn or canola

---

1 Set the water temperature to 135°F. Season the pork evenly on both sides with the table salt and pepper. Place the pork chops in the bag and then seal the bag. When the water reaches temperature, place the bagged pork in the water.

2 After 1 hour 30 minutes, remove the bagged pork from the water. Remove the pork from the bag and discard the juices. Pat the pork chops dry with paper towels and sprinkle with the coarse salt and a few grinds of black pepper.

3 Brown the pork: Heat the vegetable oil in a large skillet over medium-high heat until shimmering, about 1 minute. (You're going to make a lot of smoke here. Turn your fan on high or do this outside; cast iron can be placed on the grill.) Gently place 2 of the pork chops in the pan and sear until browned, about 1 minute 30 seconds per side. Using tongs, lean the chops against the edge of the pan or stand them on edge to sear the fatty layer on the side, about 30 seconds.

4 Transfer the pork to a plate and cover with aluminum foil. Pour out and discard about half the fat in the pan and brown the remaining two chops.

NOTE This recipe calls for ¾-inch-thick pork chops, which get just pink from sous vide cooking and then a bit darker at the edges when seared. Searing doesn't cook the interior meat as much in a thicker chop; if you use 1-inch-thick chops and like your pork closer to medium doneness, sous vide at 140°F and finish as directed.

Pork Chops with Raisins and Saffron

In Step 1, sprinkle the pork chops with a pinch of crushed saffron threads and raisins along with the table salt and pepper. In Step 2, scrape the raisins off the pork chops into a small bowl and pour the juices into the same bowl. To serve, drizzle the pork with the juices, and sprinkle with crushed pistachios and the raisins.

Pork Chops with Apple Cider Syrup

TOTAL TIME: 1 hour 50 minutes   **ACTIVE TIME:** 5 minutes   **YIELD:** Serves 4

The pork chops cook in the sous vide bath while you make the syrup on the stovetop. The precision heat of sous vide cooking means the pork chops won't overcook.

---

1 recipe The Perfect Pork Chops (page 47)

3 cups apple cider (filtered or unfiltered)

1 large pinch of table salt

---

1 When you place the pork chops in the water bath, place the cider and salt in a small saucepan over medium-high heat. Cook the cider until bubbling, then reduce the heat to medium and continue to cook until reduced to about ½ cup, about 1 hour 30 minutes. (You'll know the cider is near this point when it has darkened significantly and its bubbles break more slowly.)

2 Adjust the heat to medium-low and continue to cook until there is about ¼ cup of thickened syrup, about 10 minutes. Drizzle each finished pork chop with about 1 tablespoon of the syrup. (Handle with care: The syrup will be extremely hot and will thicken as it cools.) If the cider is unfiltered, there will be sediment. Wait until it has cooled to just warm, then stir to redistribute the sediment.

Pork Chops with Honey-Orange Glaze

TOTAL TIME: 1 hour 45 minutes   **ACTIVE TIME:** 15 minutes   **YIELD:** Serves 4

This recipe builds on a solid base, taking perfectly cooked sous vide pork chops and pairing them with a tart-sweet citrus sauce that incorporates the natural juices from the pork.

4 bone-in pork chops, ¾ inch thick (about 2 pounds)

¾ teaspoon table salt, plus more to taste

¼ teaspoon freshly ground black pepper, plus more to taste for sauce

¼ cup freshly squeezed orange juice (from 2 oranges)

¼ cup extra-virgin olive oil

2 tablespoons honey

½ teaspoon garlic powder

1 tablespoon neutral-flavored vegetable oil, such as corn or canola

1 tablespoon red wine vinegar

2 1-inch strips orange zest

Flat-leaf parsley, for garnish

Green salad, for serving

1 Set the water temperature to 135°F. Season the pork evenly on both sides with salt and pepper.

2 In a small bowl, combine the orange juice, olive oil, honey, and garlic powder. Pour into the bag and add the pork chops. Seal the bag. Massage the bag gently to distribute the marinade.

3 When the water reaches temperature, place the bagged pork in the water. After 1 hour 30 minutes, remove the bagged pork from the water. Remove the pork from the bag, reserving the juices. Pat the pork dry with paper towels and sprinkle with salt.

4 Brown the pork: In a large skillet over medium-high heat, heat the vegetable oil until shimmering, about 1 minute. Gently place 2 of the chops in the pan and sear

until browned, about 1 minute 30 seconds each side. While they sear, use a spatula to press down gently on the chops to ensure contact with the pan. Using tongs, lean the chops against the edge of the pan or stand them on edge to sear the fatty layer on the side, about 30 seconds.

5 Transfer the pork to a serving platter and cover with foil to keep warm. Pour out and discard about half the fat in the pan, brown the remaining 2 chops, and then transfer to the serving platter.

6 Pour out the fat from the pan, reduce the heat to medium, and carefully add the juices, the red wine vinegar, and the 2 orange zest strips. (Careful! The liquid will bubble and pop when it hits the heat.) Cook, stirring frequently, until reduced by half, about 2 minutes. Season to taste with salt and pepper. Remove and discard the zest, then pour the sauce over the pork. Garnish with parsley and serve hot.

Pork Chops with Honey-Orange Glaze will keep, in an airtight container in the refrigerator, for up to 3 days.

TIP
The easy way to measure honey: First coat the measuring spoon lightly with nonstick cooking spray or rub it with an oil-slicked finger. The honey slides right out!

Carnitas-Style Pork Shoulder

TOTAL TIME: 24 hours 20 minutes   **ACTIVE TIME:** 20 minutes   **YIELD:** Serves 6

If all cooking is chemistry, it pays to understand what's going on with this pork shoulder as it transforms from hunks of meat into tender strands. Long before the 24 hours have elapsed, the pork shoulder is cooked. Why not eat it then? You could. But it takes longer to break down the collagen and breaking that down is what allows the meat to fall apart into this rich, delicious dish. It's worth the wait.

2 pounds boneless pork shoulder, cut into 2-inch cubes

1½ teaspoons table salt, plus more to taste

1½ teaspoons freshly ground black pepper

1½ teaspoons ground cumin

¾ teaspoon dried oregano

¾ teaspoon garlic powder

1 medium white or yellow onion, peeled and quartered

1 cinnamon stick (about 3 inches), broken in two

1 orange, quartered (including rind)

1 lime, quartered (including rind), plus more lime segments for serving

Corn tortillas, guacamole, and pico de gallo, for serving

1 Set the water temperature to 165°F. In a small bowl, stir together the salt, pepper, cumin, oregano, and garlic powder. Sprinkle the pork evenly with the spice mixture.

2 Place the pork in the bag. Add the onion and cinnamon sticks. Squeeze the orange and lime segments over the meat and add rinds to the bag. Seal the bag and massage it to evenly distribute the ingredients and ensure they are in a single layer.

3 When the water reaches temperature, place the bagged pork in the water. Make a lid out of aluminum foil for your container, leaving a little space for the sous vide circulator. Be sure the water level is high enough to withstand some evaporation, and check the water every so often to make sure it stays above the minimum water line.

4 After about 12 hours, use tongs to remove the bag from the water bath. Give

it a gentle shake and massage to make sure the spices are evenly distributed before placing it back in the water bath. After an additional 12 hours—for a total of 24 hours—remove the bagged pork from the water.

5 Heat the broiler to high and line a rimmed baking sheet with aluminum foil. Remove the pork from the bag, discarding the juices, onions, and other flavorings. (The juices are too bitter from the citrus rinds to use in another dish.) Place the pork on the baking sheet. Allow it to cool for a few minutes and then, with a fork or clean fingers, shred the pork. Season with salt to taste.

6 Broil the pork, carefully stirring occasionally, until crisp all over, about 5 minutes. (It may take more or less time, so check early and often. This pork has cooked for 24 hours, and you don't want it to burn because it spent 1 minute too long under the broiler.)

7 Squeeze lime juice over pork and serve hot with corn tortillas, guacamole, and pico de gallo.

Carnitas-Style Pork Shoulder will keep, in an airtight container in the refrigerator, for up to 3 days, or in the freezer for up to 3 months.

TIPS
You may need to weigh down the bag with a ramekin or some sous vide weights (see Weights, page 15) to keep it submerged. While the meat is dense enough to sink, the orange, lime, and onion may make the bag float.

Prepare the pork up to Step 4 and then refrigerate or freeze and continue with Step 5 when ready to serve. (Frozen pork will take longer to crisp in the broiler; allow up to 10 minutes, checking and stirring frequently.)

Sous Vide Pulled Pork

Nudging the flavors in a different direction produces a delicious pulled pork: Keep the salt, pepper, and cumin; eliminate the oregano, garlic powder, onion, cinnamon, orange, and lime; add 2 tablespoons dark brown sugar, 1 tablespoon Spanish (smoked) paprika, and 1 tablespoon chili powder. Place 2 tablespoons prepared yellow mustard directly in the bag. After Step 4, mix the shredded pork with your favorite barbecue sauce—start with 2 tablespoons and taste before adding more, if desired. Skip the broiling and serve it on a toasted bun with pickle spears on the side.

The Perfect Pork Tenderloin

TOTAL TIME: 1 hour 10 minutes   **ACTIVE TIME:** 10 minutes   **YIELD:** Serves 3

Lean, but not too lean. Simple to make, but elegant to serve. Flavorful with the mere addition of salt and pepper, but adaptable and versatile. Easy to find in the supermarket and stress-free to stash in the freezer. Pork tenderloin provides a simple and tasty path to dinner. Sous vide cooking makes it easy to maintain a rosy-pink center while ensuring that the pork is cooked through and the outside is nicely browned.

---

1 pork tenderloin (about 1 pound)

½ teaspoon table salt

¼ teaspoon finely ground black pepper

½ teaspoon coarse salt, such as kosher or sea salt, for finishing

½ teaspoon coarsely ground black pepper, for finishing

1 tablespoon neutral-flavored vegetable oil, such as corn or canola

---

1 Set the water temperature to 135°F. Season the pork evenly with the table salt and finely ground black pepper. Place the pork in the bag and seal the bag. When the water reaches temperature, place the bagged pork in the water.

2 Meanwhile, place the coarse salt and coarse pepper on a large plate.

3 After 1 hour, remove the bagged pork from the water. Remove the pork from the bag and roll it in the coarse salt and coarse pepper until evenly coated.

4 Heat the vegetable oil in a large skillet over medium-high heat until quite hot, about 2 minutes. (If the tenderloin won't fit in the skillet, cut it into two pieces before proceeding.) Gently place the pork in the pan and sear each side, about 4 minutes total. Slice the pork into ½-inch medallions and serve hot.

The Perfect Sous Vide Pork Tenderloin will keep, in an airtight container in the refrigerator, for up to 3 days.

Peanut-Sesame Pork Tenderloin

In Step 1, add ¼ cup smooth peanut butter to the bag, massaging it onto the pork through the bag to coat. In Step 2, reduce the coarse salt to ¼ teaspoon, eliminate the pepper, and add ¼ cup sesame seeds. In Step 3, discard the peanut butter from the bag. In Step 4, reduce the heat to medium if the sesame seeds begin to turn too dark.

Spicy Pork Tenderloin for Stir-Fry

In Step 1, replace the table salt and pepper with 2 tablespoons gochujang, spread onto the pork. In Step 2, skip rolling the pork in coarse salt and pepper; remove from the water, cool and refrigerate for using in Spicy Pork and Vegetable Udon (page 59).

Spicy Pork and Vegetable Udon

TOTAL TIME: 15 minutes   **ACTIVE TIME:** 15 minutes   **YIELD:** Serves 4

Gochujang (Korean chili paste) tempers the heat with a little bit of sweetness, while cooking the pork sous vide means that it absorbs the flavor and emerges dinner-ready. From there, a rainbow of fresh vegetables and a packet of quick-cooking noodles round out the meal. The pork has a kick but is not terribly spicy, so serving the stir-fry with gochujang means diners can customize the spice level to their preference.

1 tablespoon neutral-flavored vegetable oil, such as corn or canola

1 red bell pepper, cored and chopped into small bite-size pieces

1 cup snow peas, trimmed and halved

2 medium bok choy, chopped into bite-size pieces (see Notes)

4 scallions, green and white parts, cut thin

14 ounces udon noodles (typically 2 packets), chopped (see Notes)

1 Spicy Pork Tenderloin for Stir-Fry, juices reserved and sliced thin (page 58)

2 tablespoons oyster sauce (see Notes)

Gochujang, for serving

Crushed peanuts, for garnish

1 Heat a large skillet or wok over medium-high heat for 2 minutes. Add the oil to the skillet and wait a few seconds until hot, turn the heat to high, and then carefully add the bell pepper, snow peas, and bok choy. Using a spatula, move the vegetables around until slightly blackened and blistered, about 2 minutes, lowering the heat to medium-high if the oil begins smoking.

2 Reduce the heat to medium and add the scallions and noodles. Cook until the scallions are softened and the noodles are separated about 2 minutes. Add the pork, the reserved juices, and the oyster sauce. Reduce the heat to medium-low and stir

until the pork is just heated through, about 30 seconds. Serve hot with a dollop of gochujang and garnish of crushed peanuts.

NOTES Bok choy's crevices and leaves can harbor dirt; take extra care to rinse the nooks and crannies of the vegetable before cutting.

Chopping the noodles is optional. If you're used to slurping noodles, skip it! Udon noodles can be a little unwieldly for some people when served full length. The idea is not so much to chop them to little bits, but rather—if necessary—to slice each "brick" of noodles once or twice to make things a little easier on diners.

Oyster sauce is the ingredient that makes your stir-fry taste like something that would come out of a restaurant kitchen more than just about anything else (except maybe not having to do the dishes.) While it is possible to substitute soy sauce or a bottled stir-fry sauce, oyster sauce is really where it's at.

A Better Way to Bacon

TOTAL TIME: 8 hours 10 minutes   **ACTIVE TIME:** 10 minutes   **YIELD:** 12 ounces bacon

Sous vide bacon is a power move—not just for serving strips of bacon, although, yes, please! But also because sous vide bacon can live fully cooked in your freezer ready to be crisped and served on short notice. This makes it easy to add bacon bits to meals without much fuss. Much of the work is already done for you and there's no need to do the raw-pork dance (that is, the one where you decide what, if anything, you can touch with your bacon-y hands). Just grab a strip or two of sous vide bacon from the freezer or fridge, chop it up, and add it to a stir-fry (excellent as an accent to tofu!) or vegetable dish.

---

1 package (12 ounces) thick-cut bacon

---

1 Set the water temperature to 145°F. Place the bacon in the bag and seal the bag.

2 When the water reaches temperature, place the bagged bacon in the water. Make a lid out of aluminum foil for your container, leaving a little space for the sous vide circulator. Be sure the water level is high enough to withstand some evaporation and check the water every so often to make sure it stays above the minimum water line. After 8 hours, remove the bagged bacon from the water. Remove the bacon from the bag. (At this point, you can freeze some or all of the bacon: See Sous Vide Smarter, opposite.)

3 To crisp the bacon: Preheat a large skillet over medium-high heat until very hot, about 4 minutes. Gently place as many strips of bacon as will fit in the pan and sear the first side until well browned, about 1 minute 30 seconds. Flip the bacon and cook the other side until crisped, about 30 seconds.

4 Remove the bacon from the pan, allowing most of the grease to drip into the pan as you do, and serve the bacon hot.

A Better Way to Bacon will keep, in an airtight container in the refrigerator, crisped or not, for 7 days or in the freezer for up to 3 months.

SOUS VIDE SMARTER:

BACON IN THE BANK

To freeze some or all of the bacon: Place the strips between small sheets of wax paper or parchment paper and put them in a zip-top bag labeled "cooked bacon." Labeling the bacon "cooked" is important because the bacon, at a glance, might look raw. And while it might benefit from a bit of crisping, it is cooked. Also, how many more mystery bags do you need in your freezer? Probably zero.

Because the bacon is already cooked, the crisping is just a finishing touch and the timing and crispness are entirely up to you. Bacon can be crisped warm from the sous vide bath or cold from the refrigerator or freezer, although colder bacon will require more time.

To save the bacon fat: Let cool slightly. While the fat is still liquid, pour it through a coffee filter into a glass container with a lid. Refrigerate for up to 3 weeks. (It will turn solid as it cools.) Use it to cook eggs, make stir-fries, or toast bread in a skillet.

Cooking bacon in a bag begs the question: Can you sous vide bacon using the package in which it's sold? Maybe. Should you? That's a different question and the answer is that you probably shouldn't. First, because while I can know how my bacon is packaged, I can't know how your bacon is packaged. (And if you bought it at the butcher's, maybe it's just wrapped in paper. Definitely do not sous vide in that.) Types of plastic and paper inserts may vary between brands, so it's best to use something you know is suitable.

Kimchi and Bacon Pasta

TOTAL TIME: 25 minutes   **ACTIVE TIME:** 25 minutes   **YIELD:** Serves 3

This is a quick meal made special by the rich pungency of the kimchi and the salinity of sous vide bacon. The fact that the bacon is already cooked means you don't have to worry about running around the kitchen with raw pork on your hands. Because this takes pasta outside of the typical red- or cream-sauce groove, it's a particularly good place to use whole wheat pasta—it won't seem as out of place as it might with a conventional sauce. If you've tried whole wheat pasta and found it lacking, try another brand—texture and taste vary more widely than with traditional pasta.

8 ounces dried orecchiette, rotini, or
  farfalle pasta

4 ounces A Better Way to Bacon (page 62),
  about 5 strips

1 pound broccoli crowns

2 tablespoons unsalted butter

1 cup kimchi, packed and drained

1 pinch of freshly ground black pepper

1 Cook the pasta in a pot of boiling salted water over high heat according to package directions, tasting the pasta 2 minutes before the recommended cook time. If the pasta is soft with a very, very thin core of uncooked pasta (look at the cross-section after you bite into it), it's ready. Drain the pasta, reserving 1/2 cup of the pasta water.

2 In a wok or large skillet, cook the bacon and broccoli over medium-high heat until some of the bacon is crisped and the broccoli has slightly softened, about 5 minutes. Remove the broccoli and bacon from the pan and set aside.

3 Place the butter and kimchi in the wok or skillet over medium heat. Stir until the butter is melted and the kimchi is coated, about 1 minute. Add the pasta, bacon, broccoli, pepper, and pasta water to the kimchi. Stir over low heat to warm through, about 1 minute. Divide the pasta among bowls and serve hot.

Kimchi and Bacon Pasta will keep, in an airtight container in the refrigerator, for up to 3 days.

Spaghetti Carbonara with Bacon

TOTAL TIME: 30 minutes   **ACTIVE TIME:** 20 minutes   **YIELD:** Serves 3

Spaghetti alla Carbonara is traditionally made with pork jowl (guanciale), an ingredient worth seeking out, but one that's not available in most North American supermarkets. So why not use something that is? If you've read to the end of the recipe title, you know it's bacon. Of course, it's bacon. And of course it's sous vide bacon, that potent flavor booster that's always at the ready. Eggs that have been pasteurized sous vide eliminate the safety concerns of using raw eggs. It's a rich, trattoria-worthy dish that doesn't require much work.

---

1 pound dried spaghetti

2 tablespoons extra-virgin olive oil

6 ounces A Better Way to Bacon (page 62), about 6 strips, cut into bite-size pieces

3 Pasteurized Eggs (page 167)

1 cup, tightly packed, finely grated Parmesan cheese (about 4 ounces), plus shavings for serving

Freshly ground black pepper, for serving

Chopped parsley, for garnish (optional)

---

1 Cook the pasta in a pot of boiling salted water over high heat according to the package directions, tasting the pasta 2 minutes before the recommended cook time. If the pasta is soft with a very, very thin core of uncooked pasta (look at the cross-section after you bite into it), it's ready. Drain the pasta, reserving 1/2 cup of the pasta water.

2 Heat the olive oil in a skillet over medium heat, about 2 minutes. Add the bacon and increase the heat to medium-high. Cook, stirring the bacon occasionally, until browned, about 3 minutes. Turn off the heat and set the skillet aside.

3 Lightly beat the eggs together in a large bowl. Lightly beat in the Parmesan, bacon, and fat from the skillet to combine. Add

the pasta and stir to coat, adding enough reserved pasta water to reach the desired sauce consistency.

4 Divide the pasta among bowls. Sprinkle with the Parmesan shavings, freshly ground black pepper, and chopped parsley, if using. Serve hot.

Pasta alla Gricia

Eliminate the eggs and substitute Pecorino Romano for the Parmesan. Because there are no eggs, you might need to use a heavier hand with the pasta water to thin out the sauce a bit. Go easy on the salt in the pasta water, too (but don't skip it!); the finished dish has plenty of salt from the cheese and the bacon and no egg to dilute the saltiness. You can always add more to the finished plate if it needs it.

Lentils with Eggplant and Bacon

TOTAL TIME: 30 minutes   **ACTIVE TIME:** 20 minutes   **YIELD:** Serves 4

This recipe shows the flavoring power of a little bit of meat—bacon, in particular—even when it lets vegetables take center stage. Could you make this with—gasp!—bacon not cooked sous vide? You could, of course. But cooking the bacon sous vide ahead of time means one less thing to deal with in the moment.

---

2 medium eggplants (about 12 ounces each), cut into 1-inch cubes

3 tablespoons extra-virgin olive oil, plus more for serving

1 teaspoon dried thyme

1/2 teaspoon coarse salt, such as kosher or sea salt

1 1/2 cups green lentils, picked over to discard small bits of debris

1 1/2 teaspoons whole cumin seeds

1 lemon, cut into wedges, for serving

Walnut oil, for serving (see Note)

4 ounces A Better Way to Bacon (page 62), about 4 strips, cut into bite-size pieces and crisped

Freshly ground black pepper, for serving

Parsley or cilantro, for garnish

---

1 Preheat the oven to 425°F. Cut the eggplant into 1-inch cubes. In a large bowl, toss the eggplant cubes with 2 tablespoons of the olive oil and 1/2 teaspoon of the thyme. Place on a parchment-lined baking sheet and sprinkle with the coarse salt. Roast until the eggplant is well browned, about 30 minutes, tossing it with a spatula about halfway through.

2 Meanwhile, cook the lentils: Bring a saucepan of salted water to a boil over high heat. Add the lentils, the remaining 1/2 teaspoon of thyme, and 1/2 teaspoon of cumin seeds. Reduce the heat to medium. Simmer, stirring occasionally, until the lentils are cooked and soft but with a little resistance when you bite into them, about 20 minutes. Drain.

3 Meanwhile, toast the remaining cumin seeds: Heat 1 tablespoon olive oil in a small skillet over medium-high heat for 1 minute. Add the remaining 1 teaspoon cumin seeds and reduce the heat to medium. Toast, shaking the pan frequently, until the seeds darken, about 3 minutes. Remove the skillet from the heat.

4 In a large bowl, toss together the eggplant and the lentils. Squeeze the lemon wedges over the mixture. Then drizzle generously with walnut oil or extra-virgin olive oil. Sprinkle with the toasted cumin seeds and bacon. Garnish with parsley or cilantro.

Lentils with Eggplant and Bacon will keep, in an airtight container in the refrigerator, for up to 3 days.

NOTE Walnut oil can be pricey. But fortunately, a little of its gentle nuttiness—it doesn't taste overwhelmingly of walnuts—goes a long way. If you can swing it, it's worth trying. That said, the dish will also be great with extra-virgin olive oil. And there are lots of uses for walnut oil: Drizzle it on wild or brown rice, roasted vegetables, or fish. Or use it in place of extra-virgin olive oil in finishing just about any dish. Combine it with fresh lemon juice and a small dollop of mustard for a bright, nutty vinaigrette.

Lentils with Eggplant, Bacon, and Eggs

Crack 2 Perfectly Poached Eggs (page 156) over the eggplant and lentils before topping with the bacon, cumin, and thyme.

Simply Salt and Pepper Pork Ribs

TOTAL TIME: 24 hours 15 minutes   **ACTIVE TIME:** 15 minutes   **YIELD:** Serves 4

A pronounced bite of black pepper keeps things interesting with these ribs, while the simplicity of the flavor and preparation makes it a go-to recipe. These ribs are great served with a side of roasted squash or a simple green salad. If you want to jazz things up a bit without much effort, try the thyme and garlic variation.

2½ pounds pork back ribs (see Sous Vide Smarter, page 73)

1¾ teaspoons table salt

2½ teaspoons freshly ground black pepper

Green salad, for serving

---

1 Set the water temperature to 155°F. Season the ribs evenly on both sides with salt and pepper. Place the ribs in the bags and seal the bags. (Because the rack of ribs will be longer than your plastic bags, you'll need to cut the ribs in two or even three lengths to keep them in a single layer. No problem. Just split the rest of the ingredients between/among the bags. The cook time stays the same.)

2 When the water reaches temperature, place the bagged pork in the water. Make a lid out of aluminum foil for your container, leaving a little space for the sous vide circulator. Be sure the water level is high enough to withstand some evaporation and check the water every so often to make sure it stays above the minimum water line. After 24 hours, remove the bagged pork from the water.

3 Heat the broiler to high and line a rimmed baking sheet with aluminum foil. Remove the pork from the bag, discarding the juices. Place the ribs on the baking sheet. Broil the ribs until browned, about 3 minutes. Turn the ribs over and broil about another 3 minutes to brown the other side. (It may take more time, so check early and often. You don't want your hard work—well, the sous vide circulator's hard work—to burn.)

4 Serve the ribs hot.

Thyme and Garlic Pork Ribs

In Step 1, reduce the pepper to 1/2 teaspoon and add 11/4 teaspoons garlic powder and 21/2 teaspoons dried thyme.

SOUS VIDE SMARTER:
KNOW YOUR RIBS

You will find pork ribs in different cuts. Any of the cuts will work here, though there are some differences:

Spareribs: Less meat but arguably more taste than other cuts

St. Louis-style: Similar to spareribs but trimmed further of bone and cartilage

Back or baby back: Smaller and perhaps fattier (which can mean more flavorful)

Country-style: Generally more meat and less fat

BBQ Pork Ribs with Crunchy Coleslaw

TOTAL TIME: 25 minutes **ACTIVE TIME:** 25 minutes **YIELD:** Serves 4

For me, a mayonnaise-based coleslaw lands a little too heavy to pair with a slab of ribs, though I am probably objectively wrong about this and expect an avalanche of mail telling me so. A ketchup-based barbecue sauce comes together quickly and tastes delicious, but I can accept that I'm probably wrong about that too. (Good news: It's easy to substitute your favorite barbecue sauce, whether homemade or store-bought.)

---

2 cups ketchup

1 tablespoon Worcestershire sauce

1 tablespoon chili powder

¼ cup balsamic vinegar

1 small onion, finely chopped

2 medium cloves garlic, finely chopped

1 tablespoon Dijon mustard

1 tablespoon white vinegar

1 tablespoon celery seeds

2 teaspoons sugar

¼ cup neutral-flavored vegetable oil, such as corn or canola

¼ teaspoon table salt, plus more to taste

½ teaspoon freshly ground black pepper, plus more to taste

1 bag (14 ounces) coleslaw mix (7 cups) (see Notes)

1 recipe Simply Salt and Pepper Pork Ribs, prepared through Step 2 (page 71)

---

1 Preheat the broiler. In a saucepan, combine the ketchup, Worcestershire sauce, chili powder, balsamic vinegar, onion, and garlic. Cook over medium heat, stirring frequently. If the sauce starts to bubble, turn the heat to medium-low. Cook until the onion and garlic have lost their raw edge, about 10 minutes.

2 Meanwhile, make the coleslaw: In a large bowl, whisk the mustard, white vinegar, celery seeds, sugar, oil, salt, and pepper.

Add the coleslaw mix and toss to coat. Set aside.

3 Place the ribs on a foil-lined baking sheet. Brush one side of the ribs evenly with a thick layer of sauce. Place the ribs under the broiler, sauce side up, and cook until the sauce and meat starts to brown, about 3 minutes. (Keep a close eye; broilers vary tremendously in intensity.)

4 Remove the ribs from the broiler, brush them lightly with barbecue sauce, and let them rest until cool enough to grasp with hands, about 3 minutes. Serve the ribs hot with the coleslaw and abundant napkins.

NOTES You can also try poppy or chia seeds in place of celery seeds.

Look for coleslaw mix, typically a combination of shredded cabbage (often mixed varieties) and carrots, in the produce section near the bagged salad greens. Some varieties have even more vegetables incorporated, such as a broccoli or cauliflower.

TIP

Extra barbecue sauce will keep, in an airtight container in the refrigerator, for up to 2 weeks or in a zip-top bag in the freezer for up to 3 months. Brush it on sous vide chicken or pork before finishing it under the broiler.

CHAPTER 4

Beef

No more poking at the meat, no more cutting a slit to peek, no more crossed fingers—sous vide cooking eliminates the guesswork on doneness. Whether it's a simple and tasty flank steak, beautifully tender short ribs, or an elevated and succulent filet mignon, sous vide cooking is your route to doing it right every time.

Skirt Steak with Arugula and Feta Cheese and
Anchovy Butter and Baguette (page 81)

Simple Sous Vide Skirt Steak

TOTAL TIME: 1 hour 40 minutes   **ACTIVE TIME:** 10 minutes   **YIELD:** Serves 3

This flavorful cut retains its characteristic chew while being cooked to perfection. Such a thin cut of beef cooks quickly and—more importantly—overcooks quickly. A temperature of 133°F yields a quite rare piece of beef. The finishing step on either the stovetop or grill gives it not only a bit of browning, but also the extra nudge it needs toward medium-rare. (For something closer to medium or medium-well, give the meat about 1 minute extra per side in the finishing step.)

1 pound skirt or flank steak (see Notes, page 80)

1 teaspoon table salt

½ teaspoon freshly ground black pepper, plus more to taste

1 tablespoon extra-virgin olive oil

½ teaspoon coarse salt, such as kosher or sea salt

1 tablespoon neutral-flavored vegetable oil, such as corn or canola

1 Set the water temperature to 133°F. Sprinkle the steak evenly on both sides with the table salt and pepper.

2 Place the steak in the bag and pour in the olive oil. Seal the bag and massage the steak to coat it evenly in oil.

3 When the water reaches temperature, place the bagged steak in the water. After

1 hour 30 minutes, remove the steak from the water. Remove the steak from the bag. Pat the steak dry with paper towels and sprinkle with the coarse salt.

4 Heat the vegetable oil in a large skillet over medium-high heat until just starting to smoke, about 2 minutes. Gently place the steak in the pan and sear it until browned, about 1 minute 30 seconds each side. (If

the steak won't fit in the skillet, cut it into two or three pieces.) While it sears, press down gently on the steak to ensure contact with the pan.

5 Transfer the steak to a cutting board and slice it across the grain (see Tip). Serve hot.

Simple Sous Vide Skirt Steak will keep, in an airtight container in the refrigerator, for up to 3 days.

NOTES Skirt steak (and flank steak) may need to be trimmed of "silver skin," the translucent membrane sometimes still attached. It won't hurt you, but it's not great for eating. Ask the butcher to remove it for you or remove it yourself: Use a small, sharp knife to lift up one small corner of the membrane. Grab the corner with your fingers and pull upward. Use the knife to continue separating the membrane from the meat as you continue to pull it off.

Because skirt steak is a long, thin cut of meat, it may be easiest to slice the meat into two portions and then season and bag the portions separately. The cooking time remains the same.

TIP

To determine the grain of the meat, look for parallel lines of muscle fiber. Slicing across those fibers rather than along them means a more pleasing texture in the steak. If it's difficult to tell the direction of the fibers by examining the uncut steak, make one slice (for the chef) and then adjust your cut direction if necessary.

4 IDEAS FOR SIMPLE SOUS VIDE SKIRT STEAK

Skirt Steak with Salt and Pepper Fingerling Potatoes

Prep Note: Prepare the steak through Step 3.

About 20 minutes before the steak is ready, place 1½ pounds of baby fingerling potatoes (about 3 inches long) in a large saucepan. Add enough cold water to cover them. Bring them to a boil over high heat and salt the water generously. Reduce the heat to medium-high and cook until the potatoes are tender, about 10 minutes. When the steak is ready, sear and slice. Drain the potatoes and let cool slightly, about 2 minutes. Transfer to an extra-large bowl. Add 2 tablespoons extra-virgin olive oil, 1 teaspoon coarse salt, and 1 tablespoon coarsely ground fresh black pepper. Toss gently. Season to taste or serve with Anchovy Butter (below, right). Serve with sliced steak. Serves 4.

Skirt Steak with Curried Cauliflower Puree

Prep Note: Prepare the steak through Step 3.

About 15 minutes before the steak is ready, place 1½ pounds of cauliflower florets (from one 2-pound cauliflower) into ¾ cup of boiling lightly salted water in a medium-size saucepan over medium heat. Cover and cook until tender, about 8 minutes. Drain the cauliflower, reserving the cooking water. Transfer the cauliflower to the bowl of a food processor, and add ¼ cup of the cooking water, 2 tablespoons of heavy cream, 2 tablespoons of unsalted butter, 1 teaspoon of curry powder, and ¼ teaspoon each of table salt and freshly ground black pepper. Process until the cauliflower is homogenous and creamy, about 10 seconds. Season to taste. When the steak is ready, sear and slice. Serve with cauliflower puree. Serves 4.

Skirt Steak with Arugula and Feta Cheese

Prep Note: Prepare the steak through Step 3.

About 10 minutes before the steak is ready, place 5 ounces of baby arugula (about 6 cups firmly packed) on a large serving platter. Sprinkle 4 ounces of feta or blue cheese, crumbled (about ¾ cup). Top with 1 small bunch of radishes, thinly sliced. In a small jar with a lid, combine ¼ cup of extra-virgin olive oil, 1½ tablespoons of red wine vinegar, 1 teaspoon of yellow mustard, and a generous pinch each of table salt and freshly ground black pepper. Shake to combine. When the steak is ready, sear and slice. Pour vinaigrette over the salad. Arrange the sliced steak on top of the salad and serve. Serves 4.

Skirt Steak with Anchovy Butter and Baguette

Prep Note: Prepare the steak through Step 5.

While the steak cooks, in a medium bowl, combine ½ cup of room-temperature unsalted butter; 6 anchovies packed in oil, drained and finely chopped; and a squeeze of lemon juice. Using a fork or hand blender, mix until smooth. Season to taste with coarse salt. When steak is ready, sear and slice. Spread the butter on crusty baguette torn into rough pieces and serve with steak. Serves 4. Store leftover butter in the refrigerator in a covered glass container.

Spiced Skirt Steak with Magic Mashed Potatoes

TOTAL TIME: 1 hour 10 minutes   **ACTIVE TIME:** 30 minutes   **YIELD:** Serves 4

Let me reveal the magic to these mashed potatoes right off the bat: mayonnaise. Just a little. Okay. And chicken broth concentrate. Again, just a little. Those two flavor-packed components are the magic you don't see. The magic you *do* see is the contrasting crunch to the smooth mashed potatoes, sprinkled over top. There are a few ways you can go here, and if you want to go all out, you can even make a bunch of crunch options and offer people a choice, à la crunch bar.

PREP NOTE: Prepare the steak as directed for Simple Sous Vide Skirt Steak, seasoning the steak with 1 teaspoon ground cumin and 1 pinch of cayenne pepper along with the 1 teaspoon table salt and ½ teaspoon freshly ground black pepper in Step 1.

---

1 recipe Simple Sous Vide Skirt Steak (page 79), prepared through Step 3; see Prep Note

2 pounds small baking potatoes (about 6 potatoes), such as Idaho or Russet, peeled and quartered or halved into equal-size pieces

1 tablespoon table salt

½ cup whole milk

1 teaspoon chicken broth concentrate, such as Better Than Bouillon

3 tablespoons salted butter, room temperature

2 tablespoons mayonnaise

1 tablespoon neutral-flavored vegetable oil, such as corn or canola

Mashed Potato Crunch (see box, opposite)

---

1 After the steak has cooked in the water bath for about 1 hour, place the potatoes in a pot and cover with 1 inch of water. Add the salt. Bring to a boil, then turn down the heat to maintain a vigorous simmer. Cook the potatoes until soft, about 15 minutes. To test doneness, pierce a potato with a very sharp knife; the knife should slide in easily.

(But don't poke too much, which leaves the potatoes waterlogged.)

2 Meanwhile, warm the milk in the microwave, about 10 seconds. It shouldn't be hot, just warm. Using a fork, beat the chicken broth concentrate into the milk.

3 When the potatoes are done, turn off the heat, and drain. Return the potatoes to the still-warm pot and shake the pot occasionally for about 1 minute, allowing any residual moisture to evaporate. Mash the potatoes well or pass them through a food mill.

4 In the pot with the heat on very low, stir in the butter and mayonnaise. Stir in the warmed milk mixture, half at a time, until the potatoes are smooth and creamy. Keep warm over very low heat while you finish preparing the steak. (If the mashed potatoes are stiff, add a splash of warm milk and stir it gently into the potatoes to loosen them.)

5 Finish the steak as directed in Steps 4 and 5 of Simple Sous Vide Skirt Steak.

6 Serve hot with the mashed potatoes topped with Mashed Potato Crunch, below.

Spiced Skirt Steak with Magic Mashed Potatoes will keep, in an airtight container in the refrigerator, for up to 3 days.

MASHED POTATO CRUNCH

For crunch, try one (or all) of these options:

Crispy fried onions: The kind that come in a can and are dangerously easy to snack on.

Fried sage leaves: In a small skillet over medium heat, melt enough salted butter to come about ⅛ inch up the pan. Tear fresh sage leaves from the stems and fry in the butter, a few at a time, until crisp, about 5 seconds. Transfer to a plate lined with paper towels. To serve, gently and slightly crumble the leaves over the mashed potatoes.

Toasted nuts: In a small skillet, toast chopped pistachios, macadamias, or almonds over medium heat, shaking the pan frequently. When fragrant and slightly browned, transfer them to a plate and let cool.

Crisped prosciutto: Preheat the oven to 375°F. Place sliced prosciutto on a baking sheet lined with parchment paper, leaving room between slices. Bake until the fat turns golden and the meat is darker, about 15 minutes. Using tongs, transfer the prosciutto to paper towels to drain. (It will crisp as it cools). Gently crumble on the mashed potatoes.

Soy-Lime Flank Steak with Cilantro-Citrus Rice

TOTAL TIME: 1 hour 40 minutes   **ACTIVE TIME:** 20 minutes   **YIELD:** Serves 3

The simple sweet, salty, and tangy flavoring of the steak here makes your taste buds fire on all cylinders, while the rice takes advantage of one of my favorite tricks: using an onion (mostly water, after all) as part of the liquid for cooking rice. Add a green salad or roasted vegetable and you're all set for dinner.

---

1 lime, zested and juiced

2 tablespoons soy sauce

1 tablespoon dark brown sugar

1 pound flank or skirt steak

1 large white or yellow onion, peeled and cut into large chunks

5 medium cloves garlic

¾ cup cilantro leaves, lightly packed (from 1 medium bunch cilantro)

1 tablespoon sugar

¼ teaspoon table salt

3 tablespoons neutral-flavored vegetable oil, such as corn or canola

2 cups long-grain white rice

3 cups reduced-sodium chicken broth

½ teaspoon coarse salt, such as kosher or sea salt

---

1 Set the water temperature to 133°F. In a small bowl, combine the lime juice, soy sauce, and brown sugar. Pour in the bag and add the steak. Massage and shake the bag gently to dissolve the sugar and coat the steak. Seal the bag. When the water reaches temperature, place the bagged steak in the water.

2 After 1 hour, prepare the rice: In a food processor, combine the onion, garlic, and cilantro with the sugar, table salt, and lime zest. Puree until smooth.

3 Heat 2 tablespoons vegetable oil in a medium-size saucepan with a lid over medium heat, about 1 minute. Add the rice and cook, stirring occasionally, until shiny, about 2 minutes. Stir in the pureed onion mixture, reserving 1 tablespoon for serving, and cook until fragrant and well incorporated, about 2 minutes.

4 Add the chicken broth to the saucepan and bring it to a boil over medium-high heat, about 8 minutes. Once the broth is boiling, cover the saucepan and immediately reduce the heat to medium-low. Cook until the liquid is absorbed, about 20 minutes. (You can peek—very quickly!—to see how the rice is doing, but wait at least 15 minutes before the first peek and then continue cooking if necessary.)

5 Remove the saucepan from the heat. Stir in the 1 tablespoon reserved onion mixture, making sure to incorporate it evenly. Replace the lid and leave it slightly ajar to let steam escape while you finish preparing the steak.

6 After 1 hour 35 minutes total, remove the steak from the water. Remove the steak from the bag, pat dry with paper towels, and sprinkle with the coarse salt.

7 Finish the steak

On the stove: Heat the remaining 1 tablespoon vegetable oil in a large skillet over medium-high until just starting to smoke, about 2 minutes. Gently place the steak in the pan and sear it until browned, about 1 minute 30 seconds per side. (If the steak won't fit in the skillet, cut it into two or three pieces.) While it sears, use a spatula to gently press down on the steak to ensure contact with the pan.

On the grill: Brush the clean grill grates with the vegetable oil. (If you don't have a brush, use tongs to wield a paper towel dipped in the oil.) Heat one side of the grill over high heat. When the grates are very hot, turn the heat down to low and place the steak on the grates until it picks up grill marks, about 1 minute. While it grills, use a spatula to press down gently on the steak to ensure contact with the grates. Turn the steak and repeat on the other side.

8 Place the steak on a cutting board and slice it across the grain. Serve hot with rice and a green salad.

Soy-Lime Flank Steak with Cilantro-Citrus Rice will keep, in an airtight container in the refrigerator, for 2 days.

Simply Perfect Sous Vide Sirloin

TOTAL TIME: 1 hour 10 minutes   **ACTIVE TIME:** 5 minutes   **YIELD:** Serves 2

This recipe brings utterly classic steakhouse flavor to your table with a few simple ingredients and, of course, the crucial element of sous vide cooking. The subtly hot, salty, familiar elements of Montreal steak spice complement the beef to perfection. It's often available ready-made in the spice aisle, but if you can't find it, it's easy enough to make your own (see Note). This recipe yields a steak that is medium-rare verging on medium. It is, to me, perfect. If you would like your steak closer to medium, set your sous vide circulator to 142°F. When it comes time to finish the steak, you're going to do it in a cast-iron pan, which will make a lot of smoke. Turn your fan on high or do this outside; cast iron can be placed on the grill.

---

12 ounces sirloin steak, about 1 inch thick

½ teaspoon table salt

½ teaspoon freshly ground black pepper

2 tablespoons unsalted butter

2 teaspoons Montreal steak seasoning (see Note)

---

1 Set the water temperature to 137°F. Sprinkle the steak evenly on both sides with the salt and pepper. Place the steak in the bag with 1 tablespoon of butter. Seal the bag.

2 When the water reaches temperature, place the bagged steak in the water. After 1 hour, remove the bagged steak from the water. Carefully open the bag. Pour off and discard the liquid. Using tongs, transfer the steak to a cutting board. Blot the steak with paper towels on all sides to dry the surface.

(This is the key to developing a nice crust.) Place the steak seasoning on a plate and dip both sides of the steak in the seasoning. (It's okay if not every speck sticks to the steak.)

3 Melt 1 tablespoon of butter in a large cast-iron or other heavy skillet over high heat. When the butter sizzles and starts to smoke, about 2 minutes, add the steak to the pan. Brown the first side of the steak, about 1 minute. Using tongs, turn the steak, reduce the heat to medium-high, and brown the

other side, about 1 minute more. (If there's a strip of fat on one side, use tongs to hold the steak with the fat touching the pan and cook the fat until browned, about 15 seconds.)

4 Transfer the steak to a cutting board, and then slice it in half. Serve hot.

Simply Perfect Sirloin is best served immediately after preparing.

NOTE Look for Montreal steak seasoning in the spice aisle or create your own: Combine 2 tablespoons black peppercorns, 1 tablespoon mustard seeds, 2 teaspoons dill seeds, and 1 teaspoon coriander seeds in a skillet over medium heat. Cook until the seeds begin to pop and become fragrant, about 2 minutes. Transfer the spices to a small zip-top plastic bag and crush them with a heavy skillet or pound them with a rolling pin. Add 1 tablespoon kosher salt, 1 tablespoon dried minced garlic, 1 tablespoon dried minced onion, and 1 teaspoon crushed red pepper flakes.

Use the skillet or rolling pin to crush the spices again and shake the bag to combine. Store at room-temperature in an airtight container for up to 1 month.

TIPS

Be a rebel: Try Montreal steak seasoning on chicken, pork, or roasted vegetables.

Substitute the sirloin with a 1-inch-thick T-bone, strip loin, ribeye, or porterhouse.

Sirloin with Balsamic, Soy Sauce, and Honey

In Step 1, eliminate the salt, pepper and butter. Place 1 tablespoon of balsamic vinegar, 1 tablespoon soy sauce, 1 teaspoon of toasted sesame oil, and 1 teaspoon of honey in the bag with the steak and massage the bag gently to distribute the sauce. In Step 2, use 1/2 teaspoon sesame seeds and 1/2 teaspoon coarse salt in place of steak seasoning.

Steakhouse Sirloin with Mushroom Sauce

TOTAL TIME: 15 minutes   **ACTIVE TIME:** 15 minutes   **YIELD:** Serves 2

With the right recipe, there's a lot of flavor to unlock with the basic button mushroom. Might I immodestly suggest that this is the right recipe? A good amount of butter paired with the umami of soy sauce and Worcestershire sauce elevates the humble mushroom to star side dish.

PREP NOTE: Prepare Simply Perfect Sous Vide Sirloin (page 86) through Step 2.

---

2 tablespoons unsalted butter

1 pound button mushrooms, sliced about ¼ inch thick

1 teaspoon dried basil

¼ teaspoon dried oregano

¼ teaspoon garlic powder

1 tablespoon soy sauce

Dash of Worcestershire sauce

Simply Perfect Sirloin (page 86); see Prep Note

---

1 Heat the butter in a large skillet over medium-high heat until just melted, about 1 minute. Add the mushrooms and cook, stirring occasionally, until they start to soften, about 5 minutes.

2 Reduce the heat to medium. Add the basil, oregano, garlic powder, soy sauce, and Worcestershire sauce. Cover the skillet and cook, shaking the skillet occasionally, until the spices and sauces are absorbed and distributed, about 2 minutes.

3 Open the bag with the steak and pour the juices into the skillet with the mushrooms. While finishing the steak as directed in Simply Perfect Sirloin (see page 86),cook the mushrooms, uncovered, on medium heat until most of the liquid is evaporated. Serve the steak hot with the mushrooms on top and spilling over its edges.

Filet Mignon with Horseradish Butter

TOTAL TIME: 1 hour 15 minutes   **ACTIVE TIME:** 15 minutes   **YIELD:** Serves 2

The texture of a well-cooked filet mignon is often compared to butter, tender and yielding. What more natural companion, then, than butter itself? The richness of the butter highlights and complements the richness of the beef, seasoned simply with salt and pepper. Here, the filet mignon is prepared medium-rare. It's a special-occasion meal decadent in its simplicity, with a tiny bit of horseradish for an extra kick.

---

2 filets mignons, 1½ inches thick (about 6 ounces each; see Note)

½ teaspoon table salt

½ teaspoon freshly ground black pepper, plus more to taste

3 tablespoons unsalted butter, cut into 3 pats

½ teaspoon coarse salt

¾ teaspoon prepared horseradish

---

1 Set the water temperature to 135°F. Sprinkle the filets with the table salt and pepper. Split 1 pat of butter and place half of it atop each filet. (The remaining 2 pats of butter will be used later to finish the steaks.) Seal the bag.

2 When the water reaches temperature, place the bagged filets in the water. After 1 hour, remove the bagged filets from the water.

3 Carefully open the bag and pour off the liquid into a ramekin. Using tongs, remove the filets and carefully place them on a cutting board. Blot the filets with paper towels on all sides to dry the surface. (This is the key to developing a nice crust in the next step.) Place the coarse salt on a plate and dip one side of each filet in the salt.

4 Melt the remaining 2 tablespoons of butter in a large heavy skillet over high heat until sizzling, about 2 minutes. Add

the filets to the pan, and then reduce the heat to medium-high. Cook until browned, 1 minute each side.

5 Transfer the filets to a serving platter and cover them with foil to keep warm. Let rest while you make the sauce.

6 Remove all but about 1 tablespoon of the butter from the pan. Pour the beef drippings from the ramekin into the pan over medium-high heat. Bring to a low boil, about 1 minute. Remove the pan from the heat and stir in the horseradish.

7 Drizzle filets with the sauce and serve hot.

Classic Sous Vide Filet Mignon with Horseradish Butter is best served immediately after preparing.

NOTE Filet mignon comes from beef tenderloin, so you may see this cut labeled tenderloin or tenderloin steaks.

Filet Mignon with Brandy-Shallot Sauce

Eliminate the horseradish. In Step 6, cook ½ cup finely chopped shallots (from about 3 medium shallots) with the drippings and the 1 tablespoon of butter until softened and just browned, about 5 minutes. Add 2 tablespoons brandy and the leaves of 2 sprigs of fresh thyme and continue to cook, stirring often, until most of the liquid is cooked off, about 2 minutes. Pour the sauce over the steaks and serve.

COMPOUND BUTTERS

Butter makes a great canvas for a range of ingredients and tastes. Flavored or "compound" butters take advantage of that by building one sublime servable, spreadable package. Make one of these butters while the filets cook and use in place of the horseradish butter. These are also excellent on many vegetables, such as Simple Sous Vide Carrots (page 177) and Perfect Sous Vide Asparagus (page 179).

Place 4 tablespoons softened unsalted butter in a small bowl and add one of the following:

- ¼ teaspoon minced garlic (from 1 small clove) and 1 teaspoon minced shallot (from ½ small shallot)

- ½ teaspoon ground cumin and finely grated zest of 1 lime

- 1½ teaspoons freshly and coarsely ground black pepper

- ½ jalapeño, stemmed, seeded, and minced

- 1 teaspoon shichimi tōgarashi

Mix together with a fork until incorporated. Mix in a pinch of kosher salt and taste, adding more if desired.

Serve the compound butter at room temperature or transfer it to a sheet of waxed paper or parchment paper and roll the butter into a 4-inch-long cylinder. Store it in a covered container in the refrigerator and use within 5 days or place it in a plastic bag and freeze it for up to 3 months.

Simply Sublime Sous Vide Short Ribs

TOTAL TIME: 36 hours 45 minutes   **ACTIVE TIME:** 45 minutes   **YIELD:** Serves 4

This is not a recipe for those who fear commitment; you're on the hook for about 36 hours here. But it's oh-so-worth-it. Simple, straightforward flavors start building with a quick sear before the ribs even swim in the water bath. The aromatics cook during that pre-sear, too—without that, they would never cook, even in the long (very long) and slow sous vide cook. This is a showcase recipe for the power of sous vide cooking, turning an often-tough cut of meat into one that yields easily to the fork and makes the mouth water. I suggest serving it over mashed potatoes or polenta.

2 pounds English-cut beef short ribs

1 teaspoon table salt

1 teaspoon freshly ground black pepper

1 tablespoon neutral-flavored vegetable oil, such as corn or canola

1 medium white or yellow onion, finely chopped

2 large cloves garlic, finely chopped

½ cup dry red wine, such as Cabernet Sauvignon or Tempranillo, plus a little more for the sauce

2 tablespoons Dijon mustard

1 Set the water temperature to 145°F. Sprinkle the short ribs evenly all over with the salt and pepper.

2 Heat a skillet with the vegetable oil over medium-high heat until the oil is shimmering, about 2 minutes. (Avoid cast iron here; you'll be using wine later and the mingling of the two might lead to unpleasant flavors.) Carefully place the short ribs in the skillet. Brown on all sides, turning about every 2 minutes. Transfer the ribs to a plate and set aside.

3 Reduce the heat to medium. Add the onion and garlic to the skillet and sauté for about 1 minute, stirring frequently. Add the wine to the skillet and cook until most of the liquid has evaporated, about 15 minutes. Turn the heat off.

4 Spread the ribs with the mustard, and then scrape the onions from the skillet onto the ribs. Transfer everything to the bag and seal the bag.

5 When the water reaches temperature, place the bagged ribs in the water. After 36 hours(!), remove the bagged ribs from the water.

6 Remove the ribs from the bag and set aside on a plate. Pour the liquid into a large skillet over medium heat. Add a splash of wine to the skillet and cook the sauce until the alcohol has evaporated and the sauce has thickened slightly, about 5 minutes. Gently place the ribs in the skillet and turn to coat them in the sauce.

7 Serve the ribs hot, drizzled with the sauce from the pan.

Simply Sublime Sous Vide Short Ribs will keep, in an airtight container in the refrigerator, for up to 3 days.

SOUS VIDE SMARTER:
PLAN AHEAD

There are two ways to make this an evening meal:

• Start the ribs the morning of the day before you plan to serve them.

• Start the ribs two evenings before you plan to serve them, quickly chill and refrigerate them after Step 5, and then put them in a sous vide bath at 140°F for about 20 minutes to warm them before proceeding with the rest of the recipe.

Korean-Style Short Ribs

TOTAL TIME: 8 hours 20 minutes   **ACTIVE TIME:** 20 minutes   **YIELD:** Serves 4

You have to love that such a simple recipe is so flavorful. While Korean galbi-style ribs are typically marinated before cooking, the sous vide technique allows us to essentially marinate the meat *while* we're cooking. The result is chewy, flavor-packed meat that tastes like you toiled over the stove, even while you put your feet up. They're ready to eat right out of the sous vide bag, but if you'd like, finish them on the grill. (See "On the Barbecue," page 19.)

½ cup soy sauce

¼ cup light or dark brown sugar, packed

1 medium Asian pear, peeled and grated (about ½ cup, packed)

1 tablespoon white vinegar

1 tablespoon toasted sesame oil

2 teaspoons garlic powder

½ teaspoon ground ginger

2 pounds cross-cut beef short ribs, no thicker than 1 inch

1 tablespoon sesame seeds

1 Set the water temperature to 165°F. In a small bowl, stir together the soy sauce, brown sugar, Asian pear, vinegar, sesame oil, garlic powder, and ginger. Pour the liquid into the bag and add the ribs. Seal the bag.

2 When the water reaches temperature, place the bagged ribs in the water.

3 After 8 hours, remove the bagged ribs from the water. Remove the ribs from the bag and let the liquid drain off of them (see Tip).

4 Sprinkle the ribs with the sesame seeds and serve hot.

Korean-Style Short Ribs will keep, in an airtight container in the refrigerator, for up to 3 days.

TIP
Save the liquid in the refrigerator for up to 3 days or in the freezer for up to 3 months. Brush it on squash when roasting, use it to flavor rice, or to add depth of flavor and body to soups.

Beef Short Ribs with Chimichurri

TOTAL TIME: 24 hours 30 minutes   **ACTIVE TIME:** 30 minutes   **YIELD:** Serves 4

You may naturally ask yourself if a recipe that takes 24 hours (and 30 minutes) is worth the time. The short answer is yes. The longer answer is that you know you won't be watching the ribs cook that whole time, right? A full day after the ribs go in the water, you're rewarded with a rich and tender cut of meat that eats almost like a steak. The accompanying chimichurri sauce adds a little heat and acid to the plate to cut through and complement the meat's richness. Served sliced on top of rice or polenta with a side salad, you can tell people the meal took you 24 hours or tell them it took you 30 minutes, depending on your audience. Both are true. But sometimes you want maximum drama.

CHIMICHURRI SAUCE:

¾ cup extra-virgin olive oil

½ cup red wine vinegar

½ cup finely chopped flat-leaf parsley

¼ cup finely chopped cilantro

2 tablespoons finely chopped oregano

½ teaspoon table salt

½ teaspoon red chile flakes

SHORT RIBS:

3 pounds English-cut short ribs

½ teaspoon table salt

½ teaspoon freshly ground black pepper

2 tablespoons extra-virgin olive oil

1 tablespoon red wine vinegar

2 teaspoons garlic powder

1 tablespoon neutral-flavored vegetable oil, such as corn or canola

Rice, for serving

1 Set the water temperature to 160°F. While water is coming to temperature, make the chimichurri: In a medium-size container with a lid, place the olive oil, vinegar, parsley, cilantro, oregano, salt, and chile flakes. Stir vigorously to combine, cover and refrigerate.

2 Sprinkle the short ribs evenly all over with the salt and pepper. Place the ribs, olive oil, vinegar, and garlic powder in the bag and then seal the bag. Massage the bag gently to distribute the liquid throughout.

3 When the water reaches temperature, place the bagged ribs in the water. After 12 hours, carefully lift the bag from the water, massage the bag to redistribute the liquids and return the bag to the water upside down. (It doesn't matter which side was up before; just make sure that side is down now.)

4 About 1 hour before serving, remove the chimichurri from the refrigerator, stir it, and let it stand at room temperature.

5 After 24 hours, remove the bagged short ribs from the water. Carefully open the bag and pour off and discard the liquid. Using tongs, transfer the ribs to a cutting board. Blot the beef with paper towels on all sides to dry the surface. (This is the key to developing a nice crust.)

6 Heat the vegetable oil in a large skillet over medium-high heat until it shimmers, about 1 minute. Add the ribs. Using tongs, rotate the beef every 45 to 60 seconds until browned on most sides, about 4 minutes total.

7 Transfer the ribs to a cutting board. Slice the meat into 1/2-inch strips, trimming the large pieces of fat. Serve hot, drizzled with the chimichurri.

Beef Short Ribs with Chimichurri will keep, in an airtight container in the refrigerator, for up to 3 days. At that point, leftover chimichurri should be frozen. Transfer to a quart-size zip-top bag, label it, and lay it flat in the freezer. Defrost a little at a time to dress salads or to serve atop chicken, beef, or pork.

Gnocchi with Short Rib Ragu

TOTAL TIME: 24 hours   **ACTIVE TIME:** 1 hour 15 minutes   **YIELD:** Serves 4

The higher temperature here (as compared with the Simply Sublime Sous Vide Short Ribs on page 94)—even with a shorter cooking time—results in meat that shreds easily and practically melts into the sauce. Gnocchi pair so well with this hearty sauce because they can hold their own texturally when tossed with it. But you can also use any pasta that feels as special as the sauce, such as orecchiette ("little ears"), whose scooped shape holds the sauce well, or radiatori, whose ruffles and cavities—let's call them sauce traps—allow them to carry the rich, delicious ragu with every bite.

2 pounds English-cut short ribs

1 teaspoon table salt, plus more to taste

1 teaspoon freshly ground black pepper

1 tablespoon neutral-flavored vegetable oil, such as corn or canola

2 tablespoons extra-virgin olive oil

2 carrots, peeled and finely chopped (see Tip)

1 stalk celery, leaves trimmed, finely chopped

2 medium shallots, finely chopped

2 medium cloves garlic, sliced

2 tablespoons tomato paste

1 can (28 ounces) whole tomatoes

4 sprigs fresh thyme, leaves only

1 pound fresh gnocchi

Table salt, to taste

Freshly ground black pepper, to taste

Parmesan cheese, shaved, for serving

Fresh basil leaves, slivered, for garnish (optional)

1 Set the water temperature to 170°F. Sprinkle the short ribs evenly with the salt and pepper.

2 Heat a skillet with the vegetable oil over medium-high heat until the oil is shimmering, about 2 minutes. Gently place the short ribs in the skillet. Brown the ribs on most sides, turning about every 2 minutes.

3 Transfer the ribs to a plate and let cool, about 15 minutes. Place the short ribs in the bag and seal the bag.

4 When the water reaches temperature, place the bagged ribs in the water. Make a lid out of aluminum foil for your container, leaving a little space for the sous vide circulator. After 24 hours, remove the bagged ribs from the water. Place them on a cutting board and allow to cool until comfortable to handle, about 15 minutes.

5 Reserving the liquid in the bag, use a fork to shred the meat from the bones and discard large pieces of fat or chewy bits.

6 Heat the olive oil in a large heavy pot or deep skillet (avoid cast iron; it may not play well with the acid from the tomatoes) over medium heat. Add the carrots, celery, shallots, and garlic. Cook, stirring frequently, until the vegetables are softened, about 15 minutes. (If the vegetables start to brown, reduce the heat to medium-low.)

7 Reduce the heat to medium-low and add the juices from the bagged short ribs and the tomato paste. Stir to combine. Add the tomatoes and their juices. Using a potato masher or fork, gently crush the tomatoes. Add the shredded short ribs and thyme. Simmer gently on medium or medium-low heat until the tomatoes are reduced and saucy, about 30 minutes.

8 Meanwhile, start the gnocchi: Bring a pot of salted water to boiling, add the gnocchi, and cook just until they rise to the surface of the water. They will finish cooking in the sauce.

9 While the gnocchi cook, season the sauce with salt and pepper to taste. (If the tomatoes are too thick, you can steal some pasta water and very gradually add it to thin the sauce.)

10 Drain the gnocchi and add them to the sauce. Simmer until gnocchi are tender, about 1 minute. Divide the gnocchi and sauce among warm bowls. Garnish with shaved Parmesan cheese and basil leaves, if using, and serve hot.

TIP

Chopping the carrots, celery, and shallots is great work for the food processor, if you have one. Pulse the mixture and scrape down the sides of the work bowl to make sure the vegetables are evenly chopped. It's better to chop the garlic by hand; the food processor can yield small pieces that burn easily.

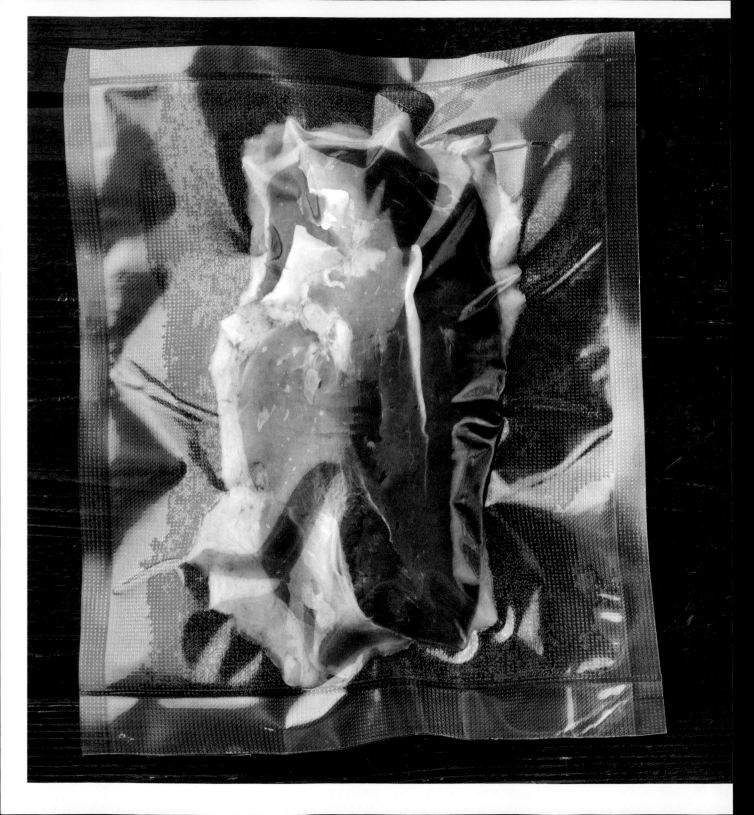

CHAPTER 5

Duck & Lamb

Duck and lamb are often served as centerpiece dishes—special occasion meats that bring us out of the ordinary with one bite. Doesn't it stand to reason that those dishes would get the attention, precision, and results that sous vide delivers? Whether with quick and simple lamb chops or a more time-consuming while still straightforward duck confit, sous vide cooking can help put something special on the table.

Simply Perfect Lamb Chops

TOTAL TIME: 1 hour 40 minutes   **ACTIVE TIME:** 10 minutes   **YIELD:** Serves 4

Lamb chops are a good choice when you want to step outside the ordinary without going over the top. These very simply prepared chops let the lamb take center stage, and are excellent accompanied by roasted or mashed potatoes. If you want to go beyond simple, two delicious variations allow you to switch it up with minimal effort and maximum effect.

8 lamb chops, ¾ inch thick (about 2 pounds) (see Note)

1 teaspoon table salt

½ teaspoon freshly ground black pepper

1 tablespoon neutral-flavored vegetable oil, such as corn or canola

1 Set the water temperature to 135°F. Season the lamb evenly on both sides with the salt and pepper. Place the lamb in the bag and seal the bag.

2 When the water reaches temperature, place the bagged lamb in the water. After 1 hour 30 minutes, remove the bagged lamb from the water bath.

3 To brown the lamb: Remove the lamb from the bag and discard the juices. Pat the lamb very dry with paper towels. (This is critical to developing a beautiful golden-brown crust.)

4 Heat the vegetable oil in a large skillet over medium-high heat until shimmering, about 2 minutes. Gently place the lamb in the pan and sear until browned, about 1 minute each side. Using tongs, lean the lamb against the sides of the skillet and brown the sides for about 30 seconds. Serve hot.

NOTE Lamb chops are typically available as loin chops—like little T-bone steaks—and rib chops—often likened to lollipops, with the rib bone forming the "handle." Either works here.

Lamb Chops with Pistachios and Pomegranate

Prepare the lamb chops as directed. To serve, drizzle lightly with pomegranate molasses (look for it in shops with a good selection of Middle Eastern products) and sprinkle with crushed, unsalted toasted pistachios.

Lamb Chops with Rosemary

Heat 1 tablespoon extra-virgin olive oil in a small skillet over medium heat. Add 2 cloves of garlic, finely chopped, and a sprig of fresh rosemary. Cook and stir until fragrant, about 4 minutes. In Step 1, pour the garlic, rosemary, and oil over the lamb chops before placing them in the bag. In Step 3, remove and discard the rosemary and garlic pieces before searing. Garnish with additional small sprigs of fresh rosemary.

Lamb with Garbanzo Beans and Roasted Garlic

TOTAL TIME: 1 hour 45 minutes   **ACTIVE TIME:** 15 minutes   **YIELD:** Serves 4

Roasting the garlic brings out a sweetness in contrast to the sharper flavor of raw garlic. It's a hands-off power move, at once intensifying and softening the flavor with a minimum of effort. While mint and lamb are a classic pairing, cilantro or parsley are delicious here as well. If you have them handy, a combination of the three herbs really pops.

8 lamb chops, ¾ inch thick (about 2 pounds); (see Note, page 107)

1 lemon, zested and juiced

1 small head garlic

¼ cup extra-virgin olive oil, plus 1 tablespoon

Pinch of table salt

Pinch of freshly ground black pepper, plus more for sprinkling over the beans

2 cans garbanzo beans (15½ ounces each), rinsed in a colander and drained

1 small bunch mint, leaves coarsely chopped, plus more for garnish

1 Prepare the Simply Perfect Lamb Chops (page 107) as directed, adding the zest of the lemon along with the salt and pepper.

2 Meanwhile, roast the garlic: Preheat the oven to 400°F. Peel off the papery outermost layers of the garlic skin, leaving the skin of the garlic cloves intact. Using a sharp knife, cut off the top of the head

of garlic, exposing the top of the cloves. (If some small cloves don't get exposed, that's okay.)

3 Place the head of garlic on a large square of aluminum foil. Drizzle with 1 tablespoon of the olive oil, the salt, and pepper. Wrap the garlic in the foil and place it upright on a baking sheet. Roast until the cloves

are lightly browned and quite soft, about 45 minutes. (Carefully remove the foil and poke the cloves with a sharp knife to see if they're softened.)

4 Remove the baking sheet from the oven, unwrap the garlic, and let cool enough to handle, about 15 minutes. Squeeze the cloves into a small bowl. Measure 2 tablespoons of the garlic, lightly packed. (If you come up short, it's okay; if you have extra, see Tip.) On a small cutting board, finely chop the garlic cloves.

5 Make the dressing: In a jar with a lid or in a small bowl, combine the chopped roasted garlic, the juice of the lemon, 1/4 cup of the olive oil, a pinch of salt, and a pinch of pepper. Shake or whisk until the dressing is homogenous.

6 In a large bowl, combine the garbanzo beans and mint. Add the dressing and toss well to combine. Grind some pepper over the salad.

7 Let the garbanzo beans stand to absorb the dressing until the lamb is done. Spoon any dressing at the bottom of the bowl over the lamb and garnish with mint.

TIP

Leftover roasted garlic will keep, in an airtight container in the refrigerator, for up to 3 days. Serve it warm spread over a baguette or mash it and mix it with cheese and pasta.

Simple Sous Vide Duck Breasts

TOTAL TIME: 1 hour 45 minutes   **ACTIVE TIME:** 15 minutes   **YIELD:** Serves 4

Duck breast is fundamentally different from chicken breast because ducks use their muscles to power their flight. Their breast muscles are rich in myoglobin, the protein that we typically associate with giving red meat its rosy hue. Duck breast, then, is that rare bird: a poultry dish that some argue is at its peak when served pink, medium to medium-rare.

---

2 boneless duck breasts (about 2 pounds)

2 cloves garlic, peeled and lightly smashed

1 teaspoon table salt, plus more to taste

½ teaspoon freshly ground black pepper, plus more to taste

1 tablespoon neutral-flavored vegetable oil, such as corn or canola

Coarse salt, for serving

---

1 Set the water temperature to 140°F. Place the duck breasts skin side down in a nonstick skillet over medium heat. (There's no need to preheat the skillet.) Cook until some of the fat melts into the pan and the skin turns golden, about 5 minutes. Flip the duck and add the garlic to the fat. Cook until the second side of the duck breasts loses translucence, about 1 minute.

2 Turn off the heat and place the duck on a cutting board. Rub the garlic over the non-skin side of the breasts and then discard the garlic and the fat in the skillet (or see Tip).

3 Season the duck evenly on both sides with the table salt and pepper. Place the duck in the bag and seal the bag.

4 When the water reaches temperature, place the bagged duck in the water. After 1 hour 30 minutes, remove the bagged duck from the water bath.

5 To brown the duck: Remove the duck from the bag and discard the juices. Pat

the duck very dry with paper towels. (This is critical to developing a beautiful golden brown skin.)

6 Heat the vegetable oil in a large skillet over medium-high heat until shimmering, about 2 minutes. Gently place the duck skin side down in the skillet and sear the skin until browned, about 3 minutes. Flip and cook the bottom side until just browned, about 1 minute. Using tongs, lean the breasts against the sides of the skillet and brown the sides for about 30 seconds.

7 Transfer the duck to a cutting board. Slice each breast thinly, sprinkle with a dash of coarse salt, and serve warm.

Simple Sous Vide Duck Breasts will keep, in an airtight container in the refrigerator, for up to 3 days.

TIP

In Step 2, save the garlic-flavored duck fat in the skillet and use it to roast potatoes or squash to serve with the duck.

Duck Breasts with Macadamias and Kiwi

TOTAL TIME: 20 minutes   **ACTIVE TIME:** 20 minutes   **YIELD:** Serves 4

Duck meat has an affinity for a citrusy sweetness—this is why we see duck classsically paired with orange. Here we riff on that pairing and give it a kiwi twist, taking advantage of the brilliant color and tart-sweet flavor of the fuzzy fruit. It's worth seeking out different color kiwis to make the dish really pop with both flavor and color (see Notes). This duck breast is delicious with a green salad or steamed green beans on the side.

PREP NOTE: Omit garlic from Simple Sous Vide Duck Breasts. Prepare through Step 4.

---

1 recipe Simple Sous Vide Duck Breasts (page 111); see Prep Note

Coarse salt

2 tablespoons mayonnaise

½ cup raw, unsalted macadamia nuts

1 tablespoon neutral-flavored vegetable oil, such as corn or peanut

8 kiwi fruit, peeled and diced into ½-inch pieces (see Notes)

---

1 Arrange a rack in the top third of the oven, place a cast-iron or other heavy oven-going skillet on the rack, and then preheat the broiler.

2 Remove the duck from the bag and discard the juices. Pat the duck dry with paper towels. Sprinkle the skin of each duck breast with a pinch of coarse salt. Turn over each breast and spread a thin layer of mayonnaise on the non-skin side

of each duck breast. (It's okay if you don't use the full amount.)

3 In a food processor, pulse the nuts until they are the consistency of large grains of sand, about 7 pulses, then stir in a pinch of salt. Sprinkle the nuts over the mayonnaise.

4 Using a heavy oven mitt, remove the skillet from the broiler, and then pour in the vegetable oil. Gently place the duck

breasts in the pan, skin side down, and return the skillet to the broiler. Cook until the macadamia nuts are golden and the skin is golden brown, about 30 seconds (see Notes).

5 Transfer the duck to a cutting board and thinly slice. Divide the kiwi among 4 plates, and then arrange the duck on top. Serve hot.

NOTES Look for golden or even red kiwi fruit to give the dish some extra visual punch and a twist of flavor. (While both taste a little like the typical green kiwi, golden kiwi are typically a little sweeter and red kiwi have hints of berry.)

Broilers are fickle and browning can happen quickly. If possible, place the skillet about 6 inches from the heat source. (Note that the time to adjust this is *before* the heat is on and not when the broiler is 1 million degrees.) Once the duck is under the broiler, keep a very close eye on it. Remember that the duck is cooked; you're just looking for color here. This is also a good place to employ a culinary torch if you have one; you'll be able to keep a closer eye on the browning as it happens.

Daylong Duck Leg Confit

TOTAL TIME: 24 hours 30 minutes   **ACTIVE TIME:** 30 minutes   **YIELD:** Serves 4

Every time I eat duck, I think, "Wow! I should eat more duck." Then, a year or two later, I have the same conversation with myself. For most of us, duck—duck fat especially—is going to be a special purchase. Here, the duck fat and slow sous vide cooking add a luxuriant element to the duck leg. If you have leftover duck fat, it is *the* fat for pan-frying or roasting potatoes.

2½ pounds duck legs, skin on and bone in (3 or 4 legs)

2 teaspoons table salt

1 teaspoon freshly ground black pepper

Zest of 1 orange

1 teaspoon sugar

1 teaspoon dried thyme

¼ teaspoon ground ginger

1 bay leaf

1½ cups rendered duck fat (see Notes)

1 tablespoon unsalted butter

Cooked green lentils or wild rice, for serving

Orange marmalade at room temperature, for serving

---

1 Set the water temperature to 170°F. Sprinkle the duck legs evenly all over with the salt and pepper.

2 Place the duck in the bag and scatter the orange zest, sugar, thyme, ginger, and bay leaf in the bag. Evenly distribute the duck fat in 1-tablespoon portions in the bag. Place sous vide weights or spoons in the bag to guard against floating. (All that fat can cause the bag to float.) Massage the bag gently to evenly distribute the spices and ensure the duck is in a single layer, and then seal the bag.

3 When the water reaches temperature, place the bagged duck in the water. Cover the container with aluminum foil, leaving a little space for the sous vide circulator. Be sure the water level is high enough to withstand some evaporation and check the water every so often to make sure it stays above the minimum water line.

4 After 24 hours, remove the bagged duck from the water bath. Remove the duck legs from the bag and pat them dry with a paper towel. Strain the fat through several layers of cheesecloth or a fine-mesh sieve and strain for future use. (see Notes).

5 Melt the butter in a large skillet over medium-high heat, about 2 minutes. Working in batches if necessary, place the duck legs in the skillet and sear, turning with tongs, until evenly browned and crisped, about 1 minute each side. (Handle them carefully to keep them intact; the meat is fall-off-the-bone tender, but you don't want it to fall off the bone just yet.) Repeat until each duck leg is browned. (You don't need to add more butter; there will be enough duck fat in the pan.) Serve the duck on a bed of green lentils or wild rice, with orange marmalade on the side.

Daylong Duck Leg Confit will keep, in an airtight container in the refrigerator, for up to 5 days.

NOTES If you're taking the time to make duck confit, it really is worth seeking out the duck fat. That said, if you need to round out the duck fat with something else in order to reach the 1½ cups, use extra-virgin olive oil. If you have no duck fat whatsoever and decide to make this, in a pinch you can use all extra-virgin olive oil.

The strained fat will keep, in an airtight container, for up to 6 months in the freezer. Use it to roast potatoes or other vegetables.

CHAPTER 6

Seafood

Delicate food calls for delicate cooking, and few foods are more delicate than seafood. Fortunately, few cooking methods are more delicate than sous vide cooking, when paired with low temperatures. About those low temperatures: They present several things to keep in mind. For specifics and important cautions, see Special Notes on Seafood (page 17).

Perfect Sous Vide Salmon

TOTAL TIME: 35 minutes   **ACTIVE TIME:** 5 minutes   **YIELD:** Serves 4

Wild salmon, available frozen outside of its limited season, has incomparable lushness and flavor. Such a rich flavor deserves spare treatment. Here, a simple salt and pepper treatment and low, quick cooking lets the fish stand out with its delicious simplicity at the fore—especially when served with a mildly flavored side like mashed cauliflower or potatoes. If you do want to take it in a different direction, two easy variations offer straightforward and tasty alternatives.

4 boneless, skinless wild salmon fillets (about 4 ounces each)

½ teaspoon table salt

½ teaspoon freshly ground black pepper

2 tablespoons extra-virgin olive oil

Fresh flat-leaf parsley leaves, for garnish

1 Set the water temperature to 120°F. Sprinkle the salmon evenly on both sides with the salt and pepper. Place the salmon and olive oil in the bag and then seal the bag.

2 When the water reaches temperature, place the bagged salmon in the water. After 30 minutes, remove the bagged salmon from the water.

3 Use tongs to gently remove each salmon fillet from the bag and place it on a serving plate. Garnish it with the parsley.

Perfect Sous Vide Salmon will keep, in an airtight container in the refrigerator, for 1 day. Serve chilled or at room temperature.

Salmon with Mustard Seed

In Step 1, sprinkle 2 tablespoons mustard seeds on the salmon. In Step 3, spoon the seeds and juice from the bag over the salmon before garnishing with parsley.

Salmon with Lemon and Dill

Eliminate the olive oil. In Step 1, spread ¼ cup fresh dill, large stems removed, and the zest of 1 lemon onto the salmon. In Step 3, squeeze the lemon over the salmon and garnish with more fresh dill instead of the parsley.

Simple Sous Vide Scallops

TOTAL TIME: 35 minutes   **ACTIVE TIME:** 5 minutes   **YIELD:** Serves 3

Scallops are all muscle—the part we eat is what opens and closes the scallop's shell. The larger your scallops, the more worthwhile it is to remove the little tab of flesh on the side of the scallop, which can be a little chewy. (Sometimes they're already removed. Win!) But it's no big deal if you don't—it's just as edible as the rest of the scallop.

1 pound (40 to 60 or 20 to 30) scallops (see Notes)

¼ teaspoon table salt, plus more to taste

¼ teaspoon freshly ground black pepper, plus more to taste

1 tablespoon extra-virgin olive oil, plus more for serving

1 tablespoon unsalted butter

1 Set the water temperature to 120°F. Sprinkle the scallops evenly with the salt and pepper. Place the scallops and the olive oil in the bag. Seal the bag.

2 When the water reaches temperature, place the bagged scallops in the water. After 30 minutes, remove the bagged scallops from the water.

3 Drain and discard the liquid from the bag. Use paper towels to pat the scallops dry and then season them lightly with salt and pepper on each side.

4 Heat the butter in a cast-iron or heavy-bottomed pan over high heat, about 2 minutes. When the pan is very hot, place the scallops in the pan and cook until browned, stirring occasionally, about 1 minute 30 seconds. Serve hot.

Simple Sous Vide Scallops will keep, in an airtight container in the refrigerator, for up to 2 days. Serve chilled or warmed.

NOTES Look for "dry" scallops, which means, whether fresh or frozen, they are sold without sodium tripolyphosphate, an additive that plumps up the scallop with water. You want to pay for scallop, not water.

The range of numbers, i.e., "40 to 60," tells you how many scallops there are per pound. The bigger the number, the smaller the scallops.

Green Tea Noodles and Scallops

TOTAL TIME: 15 minutes   **ACTIVE TIME:** 15 minutes   **YIELD:** Serves 4

This recipe takes advantage of the fact the scallops don't really need stovetop finishing to be delicious after their sous vide bath. They can easily be prepared the day before, cooled, stored in the refrigerator overnight, and then used as directed here.

PREP NOTE: Add 1 tablespoon minced ginger in Step 1 of Simple Sous Vide Scallops. Prepare through Step 3, then chill for up to 2 days.

---

8 ounces green tea wheat noodles (see Tips)

2 teaspoons toasted sesame oil, plus more for finishing

4 medium carrots, peeled and shredded (1 cup)

1 large yellow bell pepper, seeded and diced

6 tablespoons neutral-flavored vegetable oil, such as corn or canola

2 tablespoons rice vinegar

1 tablespoon sugar

½ teaspoon table salt

1 small clove garlic, finely chopped

2 teaspoons peeled and finely grated fresh ginger (see Tips)

½ cup roasted, lightly salted cashews (see Tips), broken into rough chunks

1 recipe Simple Sous Vide Scallops (page 123); see Prep Note

---

1 In a medium-size saucepan, prepare the green tea noodles as directed on the package, drain in a colander, and then rinse with cold water.

2 Place the noodles in a large serving bowl and toss them with the sesame oil. Add the carrots and bell pepper and toss everything to combine. (Use kitchen shears to cut some of the noodles, if desired.)

3 In a small bowl, whisk the vegetable oil, vinegar, sugar, salt, garlic, and ginger. Pour the dressing over the noodles, add the cashews, and toss again.

4 To serve, divide the noodles among plates. Using tongs, carefully remove a few scallops from the bag and place them on top. Drizzle each serving with sesame oil.

TIPS

If you can't find green tea noodles, buckwheat soba or wheat udon noodles are good choices.

Got some extra ginger? Place the whole, unpeeled piece in a zip-top freezer bag and freeze for up to six months. There's no need to thaw it before peeling and grating it.

Look for cashews that have just a dusting of visible salt and don't taste like a sodium bomb when you pop one in your mouth. Ideally, they should be *salted* without being *salty*.

Scallops with Salmon Roe and Wild Rice

TOTAL TIME: 50 minutes   **ACTIVE TIME:** 10 minutes   **YIELD:** Serves 4

These recipe ingredients, although not likely to be lurking in your kitchen, add up to a special occasion tableau on the plate: The earthiness of the wild rice meets the minerality of the seaweed, topped off with the gentle sweetness of perfectly cooked scallops, punctuated by the bursts of salinity from the beautiful pink salmon roe. It's a dish that invites you to savor the contrasts and complements in every bite.

PREP NOTE: Prepare Simple Sous Vide Scallops through Step 3, then chill for up to 2 days.

1¾ ounces (50 grams) salmon roe (see Notes)

1½ cups wild rice blend (see Notes), rinsed well in a sieve

3 cups chicken broth

3 cups water

3 sheets roasted nori (see Notes)

1 recipe Simple Sous Vide Scallops (page 123); see Prep Note

Table salt, to taste

Freshly ground black pepper, to taste

1 tablespoon unsalted butter

---

1 Place the salmon roe on the counter to take some of the chill off while you prepare the rice.

2 In a medium-size saucepan, combine the rice, broth, and water. Bring to a boil over high heat. Reduce the heat to just a simmer, and cover.

3 Meanwhile, prepare the nori: Stack the sheets on one another. Using kitchen shears, cut the sheets into about 10 strips. Stack the strips 5 at a time and cut each strip into about 10 small bite-size pieces.

4 After 45 minutes, check the rice: It should be chewy but not crunchy. If the grains are not tender, continue to simmer with the cover on for 5 minutes before checking again.

5 When the rice is cooked, turn off the heat and pour the rice into a strainer to drain the liquid.

6 Return about one third of the rice back to the still-warm pot, followed by about one third of the nori. Stir gently, and then continue alternating with the rice and nori. (Adding the nori in stages keeps the nori from clumping together when it meets the moisture in the rice.) Cover the saucepan to keep the rice warm.

7 Sear the scallops: Drain and discard the liquid from the bag. Using paper towels, pat the scallops dry and then season them lightly with salt and pepper on each side.

8 Heat the butter in a cast-iron or heavy-bottomed pan over high heat. When the pan is very hot, about 2 minutes, place the scallops in the pan and cook until browned, stirring occasionally, about 1 minute 30 seconds. (This may splatter and generate some smoke.)

9 Divide the rice among four shallow bowls, top each bowl with a few scallops, and then garnish with a spoonful of salmon roe. Serve hot.

Scallops with Salmon Roe and Wild Rice is best eaten immediately after it is prepared.

NOTES Both roasted nori (a type of seaweed) and salmon roe, or ikura, are used in preparing sushi and can be found in well-stocked fish markets, Japanese markets, or anywhere sushi ingredients are sold. You may also substitute other roe if they are more readily available—the eggs of flying fish (tobiko) are a particularly good substitute. As a substitute for roasted nori, try a few tablespoons of toasted sesame seeds for a little crunch and the same toasty notes.

Wild rice blend is available packaged or in bulk bins at well-stocked supermarkets. Look for a blend that includes both grains of wild rice and varieties of brown rice. Or make your own blend by combining about 20 percent wild rice with 80 percent long-grain brown rice.

Scallops with Grapefruit and Risotto

TOTAL TIME: 45 minutes   **ACTIVE TIME:** 45 minutes   **YIELD:** Serves 2

Some flavor combinations just work. And while you might at first cock your head at the marriage of grapefruit, scallops, and rice, this recipe pulls it all together: The citrusy sweet-sour of the grapefruit, the ocean-born, fresh salinity of the scallops, and the creaminess of the risotto add up to a trio that's almost symphonic.

PREP NOTE: Prepare Simple Sous Vide Scallops through Step 3, then chill for up to 2 days.

---

2 large red grapefruit

3½ cups water

4 tablespoons (½ stick) unsalted butter

1 small onion, finely chopped

1 cup arborio rice

4 sprigs fresh thyme, plus more for garnish

Table salt, to taste

Freshly ground black pepper, to taste

½ recipe Simple Sous Vide Scallops (page 123); see Prep Note

---

1 Finely zest and juice one grapefruit. Cut the remaining grapefruit into neat segments. (See Tip.) Set the zest, juice, and segments aside.

2 Prepare the risotto: In a small saucepan heat the water over high heat until just short of a boil. Reduce the heat to medium-low to keep warm.

3 Melt 2 tablespoons of the butter in a medium-size saucepan over medium-high heat, about 30 seconds. Add the onion and cook, stirring frequently, until just translucent, about 2 minutes.

4 Add the rice to the saucepan with the butter and onion and cook, stirring frequently, until the grains are translucent, about 2 minutes. Reduce heat to medium, add the grapefruit juice, and cook until it is absorbed, about 1 minute.

5 Add the warmed water, ½ cup at a time, stirring to incorporate each addition as the rice absorbs it. When that addition of water

is almost absorbed by the rice, add the next ½ cup of water. Continue this until the rice is creamy and quite tender, with just a little bit of resistance when you bite into it. The whole process should take 20 to 25 minutes. You might have about ½ cup of water remaining; save it to loosen the risotto later.

6 Remove the thyme leaves from the stems. Stir 1 tablespoon of butter into the risotto and add the thyme leaves. Add a large pinch of salt and a large pinch of pepper, then gradually and gently fold in the grapefruit segments. Season to taste with additional salt and pepper.

7 Reduce the heat to low, stirring occasionally, while you prepare the scallops.

8 Drain and discard the liquid from the bag. Using paper towels, pat the scallops dry and then season lightly with salt and pepper on each side.

9 Heat the remaining 1 tablespoon of butter in a cast-iron or heavy-bottomed pan over high heat. When the pan is very hot, about 2 minutes, place the scallops in the pan and cook until browned, stirring occasionally, about 1 minute 30 seconds.

10 Divide the risotto between two shallow bowls or deep plates. (If the risotto is very thick, loosen it by adding 2 tablespoons of hot water and stirring it gently until it is incorporated.)

11 Top each bowl with half of the scallops and garnish with a sprig of thyme. Serve hot.

Scallops with Grapefruit and Risotto is best eaten immediately after it is prepared.

TIP

To supreme the grapefruit: Using a large knife, slice off the bottom and the top of the grapefruit. Place it on a cutting board with one cut side down. Using a smaller sharp knife, cut the peel and pith away from the fruit, exposing the pink flesh. (If your knife is sharp, you can be conservative at first and leave some pith attached to the flesh before returning to do touch-up work.) Turn the grapefruit on its side and cut the grapefruit segments away from the membranes. Voilà!

Swimmingly Simple Shrimp

TOTAL TIME: 50 minutes **ACTIVE TIME:** 5 minutes **YIELD:** Serves 4

Cooking shrimp sous vide means combining the perfect time and temperature to yield shrimp that are tender, with a bit of a snap when you bite into them. It's worth seeking out shrimp worthy of the delicate and precise cooking method. Such shrimp can shine with salt and pepper alone, but for a simple twist, try Chile-Garlic Shrimp (page 134).

1½ pounds (20 to 40) peeled and deveined frozen shrimp (see Notes)

1 tablespoon extra-virgin olive oil

½ teaspoon table salt, plus more to taste

½ teaspoon baking soda (see Notes)

1 Set the water temperature to 135°F. Place the shrimp, the olive oil, salt, and baking soda in the bag. Seal the bag. Massage and shake the bag gently to distribute the salt throughout the bag.

2 When the water reaches temperature, place the bagged shrimp in the water. After 45 minutes, remove the bagged shrimp from the water. Drain and discard the liquid from the bag.

3 Serve hot as is, add (without further cooking) to your favorite shrimp recipe, or chill immediately in an ice bath and place in the refrigerator.

Swimmingly Simple Shrimp will keep, in an airtight container in the refrigerator, for up to 2 days. Serve chilled or warmed.

NOTES The range "20 to 40" tells you how many shrimp there are per pound. Many sizes will work here; between 12 and 60 is a good range.

The baking soda is here because of J. Kenji López-Alt, who tells us that it helps firm up and plump the shrimp. As with so many things, he's right. If the shrimp already contain sodium carbonate, sodium citrate, or sodium bisulfate—read the label—you can skip the baking soda.

Chile-Garlic Shrimp

In Step 1, in a small skillet, heat 4 tablespoons extra-virgin olive oil and 2 large cloves garlic, thinly sliced, over medium heat. Sauté, stirring occasionally, until the garlic is no longer raw but is not turning brown, about 3 minutes. Add 2 tablespoons brandy and cook until most of the alcohol is evaporated, about 2 minutes more. Finely zest 2 lemons and place the zest in the bag. (Reserve the lemons for serving.) Place the shrimp in the bag, followed by the cooked garlic with the olive oil, a pinch of red chile flakes, 1/2 teaspoon table salt, and 1/2 teaspoon freshly ground black pepper. Serve with a squeeze of lemon or incorporate into Whole Wheat Spaghetti with Shrimp and Walnuts (page 138).

QUICK DIPS

There's no need to limit yourself to traditional cocktail sauce. While the shrimp cook, consider whipping up one of these dipping sauces. They also make delicious accompaniments to scallops (see page 123).

Sriracha mayonnaise: Use a fork to combine 1/2 cup mayonnaise with 2 squirts of sriracha, taste and add more sriracha if desired.

Citrus mayonnaise: Use a fork to combine 1/2 cup of Homemade Lemony Mayonnaise (page 169) or store-bought mayonnaise with the freshly grated zest of 1 lemon, lime, orange, or grapefruit, plus 1 tablespoon freshly squeezed juice from the fruit. (If the juice of the lime doesn't quite make 1 tablespoon, don't sweat it.)

Spicy green dipping sauce: Make the Chimichurri Sauce (page 98), reducing the vinegar to 1/4 cup and salt to 1/4 teaspoon. Eliminate the oregano. Add a splash of fish sauce and a handful of finely chopped chives.

Chili Crisp Shrimp with Rice Noodles

TOTAL TIME: 30 minutes   **ACTIVE TIME:** 20 minutes   **YIELD:** Serves 4

Spicy chili crisp comes from China, and in North America it has been made a pasta garnish, a deviled egg ingredient, a trendy sundae topping, and even the subject of an article that deemed it a "cult." I don't know about it being a "cult," but, on the other hand, it has a lot of true believers. And while I might be late to the game, I am happy to count myself among the believers in this crispy, spicy, savory sauce. Here, it's layered into the dish, both cooked with the shrimp in a sous vide bath and added to the noodles on the stovetop.

PREP NOTE: Substitute 2 tablespoons spicy chili crisp for all the ingredients in Step 1 of Swimmingly Simple Shrimp. Prepare and chill for up to 2 days.

---

2 bunches scallions (see Notes)

6 tablespoons neutral-flavored vegetable oil, such as corn or peanut

½ teaspoon table salt

4 teaspoons toasted sesame oil

8 ounces rice noodles (about ¼ inch wide)

12 ounces green beans, ends trimmed and cut into 1-inch lengths

1 tablespoon spicy chili crisp sauce (see Notes)

1 recipe Swimmingly Simple Shrimp (page 133); see Prep Note

Lime, quartered, for serving

Sugar, for serving

Crushed unsalted peanuts, for garnish

---

1 Trim the roots from the scallions and cut the scallions on the bias into 1-inch pieces. Reserve ¼ cup of the scallion tops.

2 Heat the vegetable oil in a large saucepan over medium-low heat. Add the scallion pieces and salt. Cook and stir for 2 minutes. Reduce the heat to low. Cook, stirring often, until the oil is tinted green and the scallions are very soft but not browned, about 20 minutes. Stir in the sesame oil, and remove the pan from the heat.

3 Meanwhile, place the rice noodles in a large bowl of cool water to soak according to package directions.

4 Heat a large skillet or wok over medium-high heat until a drop of water dances and then disappears, about 2 minutes. Add the green beans and cook, stirring frequently, until a few little black spots appear on each bean, about 1 minute.

5 Reduce the heat to medium, place the noodles in the skillet, add ¼ cup of water (watch out for the steam), and cook until soft, about 2 minutes. (If the water evaporates and the noodles are not soft, add another ¼ cup.)

6 Place the scallions, their oil, the reserved scallion tops, the chili crisp, and the drained shrimp from the bag in the skillet and then quickly stir them into the noodles.

7 Divide the noodles among four plates. Top each with a squeeze of lime juice and a sprinkle of sugar. Garnish with a spoonful of crushed peanuts. Serve warm.

Chili Crisp Shrimp with Rice Noodles is best eaten immediately after it is prepared, but it will keep, in an airtight container in the refrigerator, for up to 2 days.

NOTES Bunches are not a standard unit of measure for scallions, of course. But we're talking big onions, here. Aim for about 12 scallions total, each 14 inches long.

Lao Gan Ma is a widely available brand of chili crisp, though others have cropped up amid the product's surge in popularity. Tao Huabi, the Chinese entrepreneur who founded the company that makes it, started by selling noodles with sauce at a market. Her company now makes more than 1 million jars of spicy chili crisp each day. Look for it where Asian ingredients are sold.

Whole Wheat Spaghetti with Shrimp and Walnuts

TOTAL TIME: 40 minutes   **ACTIVE TIME:** 15 minutes   **YIELD:** Serves 4

Whole wheat pasta has a lot going for it nutritionally, but it took me a while to fall for it because we weren't introduced properly. I spent too much time trying to make it work in the typical red and cream sauces. And, while you can do that, it benefits tremendously from treatment as a whole other animal, excelling in combinations where your taste buds aren't trained to "expect" ordinary pasta. That's where walnuts and sous vide shrimp come in. It might be outside the realm of what you think of as a typical pasta dish, but everything is better for it.

PREP NOTE: Chill the Swimmingly Simple Shrimp in the sous vide bag for up to 2 days before using in this recipe.

---

1 recipe Swimmingly Simple Shrimp, Chile-Garlic variation (page 134); see Prep Note

¾ cup walnut halves

1 pound whole wheat spaghetti

Coarse salt, to taste

Freshly ground black pepper, to taste

Fresh lemon wedges, for serving

Extra-virgin olive oil, for serving

Fresh flat-leaf parsley or basil, for garnish

---

1 Toast the walnuts: Place the walnuts in a large skillet over medium heat. Toss frequently until just starting to toast and they become fragrant, about 4 minutes. If you're not sure, it's better to err on the side of under-toasted.

2 Remove the walnuts from the heat, and reserve about half of them in a bowl. Place the remaining walnuts on a cutting board, and finely chop.

3 Prepare the pasta: Bring a large pot of generously salted water to a boil over high

heat. Break the spaghetti in half and cook according to package directions. (Check the pasta 3 minutes before the package directions indicate. It's al dente when biting into a strand reveals a very tiny core of uncooked pasta. This is what provides the bite and bounce to well-cooked pasta. Stop cooking it immediately.) Drain, reserving 1/2 cup pasta water. (The starch in the water will help thicken the sauce.)

4 Pour about half of the shrimp and juices into the skillet over medium-high heat. Add about half of the pasta and half of the walnut halves. Toss until well combined, then add the remaining shrimp and juices, pasta, and walnuts. (Combining in batches makes it easier to thoroughly mix the ingredients.) Season to taste with salt and pepper.

5 Pour the pasta into a serving dish. Squeeze lemon wedges lemon wedges over the pasta, drizzle with olive oil, sprinkle with the finely chopped walnuts, and garnish with parsley or basil. Serve hot.

Whole Wheat Spaghetti with Shrimp and Walnuts will keep, in an airtight container in the refrigerator, for up to 2 days. To serve, loosen the pasta with a bit of water and olive oil and microwave on medium until warm.

TIP

Here's another great combination: Substitute regular bucatini for the whole wheat spaghetti and pistachios for the walnuts.

Chile-Vanilla Olive Oil

TOTAL TIME: 3 hours 30 minutes   **ACTIVE TIME:** 30 minutes   **YIELD:** About 1 cup infused oil

You gotta love a recipe that begins with addressing botulism, right? It's important. Here it goes: Do not go rogue and use fresh herbs or spices here. The moisture and potential bacteria could easily lead to botulism when combined with the oxygen-free environment of the oil. (While we need air to breathe, *C. botulinum* bacteria are the opposite; they thrive in oxygen-free environments.) Store the flavored oil in the refrigerator.

Now that we've got that settled, do give this recipe a try. It's wonderful drizzled over fish, lobster, roasted squash, ice cream (vanilla, chocolate, or pistachio are good choices), Pumpkin Pie Cups (see page 207), or rice pudding. Yes, that's quite an eclectic list of serving suggestions. The gentle sweetness of the vanilla comes through first, followed by the kick from the chile. The savory options highlight the heat of the chile flakes, while the sweet options lean on the vanilla. It all works. The delicate flavors here make this best used as a finishing oil, drizzled over a plated dish.

---

1 cup extra-virgin olive oil (see Note)

1 teaspoon dried red chile flakes

1 whole vanilla bean, split and cut in half crosswise

---

1 Set the water temperature to 135°F. In a half-pint canning jar with a lid, combine the olive oil, chile flakes, and vanilla bean halves. Attach the canning lid and band to the jar and make the band fingertip tight (see Glass Jars, page 14).

2 When water reaches temperature, use heat-resistant gloves or canning tongs to place the jar in the water bath. After 3 hours, use heat-resistant gloves or canning tongs to remove the jar.

3 About 30 minutes before the oil comes out of the bath, sterilize another half-pint canning jar with lid for storing the oil: Place the freshly cleaned jar and band in a large pot of simmering water for 15 minutes. With

5 minutes left, add the lid to the water. Using canning tongs, remove the jar, band, and lid and place on a clean towel.

4 Filter the oil: Place a coffee filter over the sterilized half-pint canning jar. Pour the oil into the filter and let it to drip into the jar. Seal with the sterilized lid and band. Store in the refrigerator.

Chile-Vanilla Olive Oil will keep, in an airtight container in the refrigerator, for up to 4 days or in the freezer for up to 2 months. (It will freeze solid; leave the jar at room temperature about 15 minutes before scooping out the portion you plan to use and then bring that portion back to room temperature before serving. Return the remainder to the freezer.)

NOTE This is a good place for a middle-of-the-road olive oil—not the top-shelf, break-the-bank liquid gold, but not the bottom-of-the-barrel stuff either. The taste of the olive oil is an important component here, but you don't want it to overwhelm the other flavors.

Sweet or Savory Infused Olive Oil

Take the infused oil into decisively savory or sweet territory: In Step 1, use 1 teaspoon dried red chile flakes OR 1½ whole vanilla beans. (Without the kick from the chile, the oil benefits from a little more of a vanilla edge.)

Perfect Sous Vide Tuna Steak

TOTAL TIME: 1 hour 20 minutes   **ACTIVE TIME:** 5 minutes   **YIELD:** Serves 4

Someone pulled the fish out of the ocean for you, right? It's tempting to think the hard work stops there. But no. Shopping for tuna can mean navigating a minefield. Tuna encompasses many fish in a number of distinct fisheries, caught by a number of methods with a variety of fishing-management programs—or none at all. Just because it's for sale doesn't mean it should be sold. Overfishing of tuna and incidental damage to other species are just two of the possible issues. Yellowfin tuna is often a good bet, though the details on fishing method and location matter. Check the Monterey Bay Aquarium Seafood Watch website (seafoodwatch.org) for up-to-date, high-quality information on which tuna to choose. And then enjoy your meal.

---

1 pound tuna steak, about 1½ inches thick

½ teaspoon table salt

¾ teaspoon coarsely ground black pepper

1 tablespoon neutral-flavored vegetable oil, such as corn or canola

Coarse salt, for serving

Extra-virgin olive oil, for serving

Green salad, for serving

---

1 Set the water temperature to 105°F. Sprinkle the tuna with the table salt and let stand, at room temperature, for 30 minutes. Place the tuna in the bag and seal the bag.

2 When the water reaches temperature, place the bagged tuna in the water. After 30 minutes, remove the bagged tuna from the water.

3 Drain and discard any liquid from the bag. Using tongs, transfer the tuna to a plate. Blot the tuna dry with paper towels, and sprinkle the tuna evenly with the black pepper.

4 Heat a cast-iron or heavy-bottomed pan over high heat. When the pan has just begun to warm up, pour the vegetable oil on a corner of a paper towel and then use the paper towel to wipe a thin layer of oil onto the pan.

5 When the pan is searing hot, about 3 minutes, place the tuna on the pan and cook until charred, about 30 seconds. Turn the tuna and cook until the other side is darkened, about 30 seconds more.

6 Sprinkle the tuna with a dash of coarse salt and drizzle with olive oil before serving hot, or chill immediately in an ice bath and place in the refrigerator to serve cold later.

Perfect Sous Vide Tuna Steak will keep, in an airtight container in the refrigerator, for up to 2 days. Serve chilled in a sandwich or atop a salad.

Oil-Poached Tuna

Use a 1-quart bag. Set the water temperature to 120°F. In Step 1, place ½ teaspoon table salt, 1 cup extra-virgin olive oil, and 1 cup pure (refined) olive oil or neutral-tasting vegetable oil in the bag with the tuna. (The tuna should be completely immersed in a generous quantity of oil.) In Step 3, use tongs to carefully remove the tuna from the bag, reserving the olive oil. (Skip the searing.) To serve warm, slice the tuna and then pour a spoonful of the olive oil over it when serving. Season to taste with coarse salt and freshly ground black pepper. Or, refrigerate immediately and serve chilled in a salad or sandwich. Strain the remaining oil through a coffee filter and store, in a covered glass container in the refrigerator, for up to a week, or freeze for up to 3 months. Use it to enliven the flavor of pasta or roasted vegetables.

Tender Sous Vide Octopus

TOTAL TIME: 5 hours 10 minutes **ACTIVE TIME:** 10 minutes **YIELD:** Serves 2

Behold three methods that may yield tender octopus: 1. Cooking it with a cork—often handy but also mysterious, since explanations of how it works are hard to come by. 2. Beating it against a rock—often not a feature of modern kitchens and quite labor-intensive even if you do have one handy. 3. Cooking it sous vide—quite easy, and, as it happens, the subject of this cookbook. It's the only one I can personally vouch for.

12 ounces octopus tentacles (1 or 2 tentacles)

2 tablespoons extra-virgin olive oil, plus more for serving

¼ teaspoon table salt, plus more for serving

¼ teaspoon freshly ground black pepper, plus more for serving

1 Set the water temperature to 170°F. Place the octopus, 1 tablespoon of the olive oil, and the ¼ teaspoon each of the salt and pepper in the bag. Seal the bag.

2 When the water reaches temperature, place the bagged octopus in the water. After 5 hours, remove the bagged octopus from the water.

3 Heat a cast-iron or heavy-bottomed pan over high heat. While the pan heats, remove the octopus from the bag, blot it dry with paper towels, brush it with the remaining 1 tablespoon olive oil, and sprinkle it with a pinch of salt. When the pan is searing hot, about 3 minutes, place the octopus in the pan and cook until charred, about 1 minute 30 seconds. Flip the octopus and sear until the other side is charred, about 1 minute.

4 Sprinkle the octopus with a dash of salt and pepper, and drizzle with olive oil. Serve hot.

Tender Sous Vide Octopus will keep, in an airtight container in the refrigerator, for up to 2 days. Serve chilled.

Paprika-Spiced Octopus

In Step 1, replace the black pepper with 1 teaspoon Spanish paprika. In Step 3, brush the octopus with 1 tablespoon extra-virgin olive oil and sprinkle with ½ teaspoon paprika before finishing it in the pan.

Soy-Garlic Octopus

In Step 1, place the octopus, 1 tablespoon soy sauce, and ½ teaspoon garlic powder in the bag. In Step 3, brush the octopus with 1 tablespoon vegetable oil, such as corn or canola, and sprinkle it generously with coarse salt, such as sea salt or kosher salt, before finishing it in the pan.

Octopus with Spiced Couscous

TOTAL TIME: 30 minutes   **ACTIVE TIME:** 20 minutes   **YIELD:** Serves 4

The western Sicilian city of Trapani is about 150 miles across the sea from the Tunisian capital of Tunis. This proximity to Africa ripples into the cuisine, where couscous can jockey with pasta for primacy on the city's plates. This dish is inspired by that place, where on a part of the island that juts into the ocean you can sit down to a meal with the sea on three sides and the cuisine straddling two continents.

---

1 recipe Tender Sous Vide Octopus (page 145)

¼ cup blanched, slivered almonds

1 tablespoon extra-virgin olive oil, plus more for serving

1 small onion, finely chopped

1 clove garlic, finely chopped

1 teaspoon ground coriander

1 teaspoon ground cumin

1 teaspoon ground cinnamon

¼ teaspoon turmeric

1 cup pearl couscous

1 cup reduced-sodium chicken broth

Pinch of table salt, plus more to taste

Fresh flat-leaf parsley or cilantro, for garnish

---

1 About 30 minutes before the octopus is finished, toast the almonds: Place the almonds in a medium-size saucepan over medium heat. (Choose a saucepan that has a cover; you'll use it later.) Toss the almonds frequently until they just start to toast and become fragrant, about 3 minutes. If you're not sure, it's better to err on the side of under-toasted. Turn off the heat, pour the almonds onto a small plate, and set aside.

2 Prepare the couscous: In the same saucepan, heat 1 tablespoon olive oil over medium-high heat. Add the onion and garlic. Cook, stirring frequently, until no longer raw, about 2 minutes. Reduce the heat to medium. Add the coriander, cumin, cinnamon, and turmeric. Cook until very fragrant, about 2 minutes more.

3 Add the couscous to the saucepan and stir to combine. Add the chicken broth and bring just to a boil, about 2 minutes. Cover, reduce the heat to low, and simmer until couscous is done, about 10 minutes. Stir in the almonds, remove from the heat, and replace the cover until the octopus is ready.

4 Heat a cast-iron or heavy-bottomed pan over high heat. While the pan heats, remove the octopus from the bag and blot it dry with paper towels. When the pan is searing hot, about 3 minutes, place the octopus in the pan and cook until charred, about 1 minute 30 seconds.

Turn the octopus and sear until the other side is charred, about 1 minute. Transfer the octopus to a cutting board and cut it crosswise into bite-size pieces.

5 Divide the couscous among four plates and top each with some of the octopus. Garnish the couscous with the parsley or cilantro and sprinkle the octopus with a dash of salt and a drizzle of olive oil. Serve hot.

Octopus with Spiced Couscous will keep, in an airtight container in the refrigerator, for up to 2 days. Serve chilled.

Spaghetti with Butter-Poached Lobster Tails

TOTAL TIME: 1 hour 30 minutes   **ACTIVE TIME:** 15 minutes   **YIELD:** Serves 2

I like to make this with spaghetti alla chitarra, which is a little thicker than typical spaghetti and has squared edges. It might be a special purchase, but it's worth seeking out. If you find some, buy a few packages. It'll last for eons and is a good way to signify special-occasion pasta, even beyond this dish. Spaghettoni is a thicker version of spaghetti that has a little more chew than its slimmer sibling and also works well here.

---

2 frozen North Atlantic lobster tails (3½ to 5 ounces each) (see Note)

3 tablespoons salted butter, cut into small chunks

8 ounces spaghetti alla chitarra, spaghettoni, or fettuccine

2 medium lemons

1 large handful fresh flat-leaf parsley, large stems removed

1 large handful fresh basil, large stems removed

⅓ cup heavy cream

---

1 Set the water temperature to 140°F. Rinse the lobster tails in cold water, and then pat them dry with a cloth. (See Note.) Place the lobster tails and butter in the bag along with sous vide weights or stainless-steel spoons. Seal the bag.

2 When the water reaches temperature, place the bagged lobster in the water.

3 After 35 minutes, begin to prepare the spaghetti alla chitarra: Over high heat, bring a large pot of generously salted water to a boil. When the lobster has about 10 minutes of cooking time remaining, break the spaghetti in half and cook according to the package directions. (Check the pasta 3 minutes before the package directions indicate. It's al dente when biting into a strand reveals a very tiny core of

uncooked pasta. This is what provides the bite and bounce to well-cooked pasta. Stop cooking it immediately.)

4 Meanwhile, zest both lemons and quarter one of them. Juice the whole lemon and set the juice aside. Chop the parsley and cut the basil crosswise into thin slivers.

5 After 1 hour 15 minutes total, remove the bagged lobster from the water.

6 Pour the butter and juices from the bag, the cream, and the lemon zest into a large skillet over medium heat. Bring to a low simmer, stirring occasionally. (Reduce the heat to medium-low if it begins to show anything beyond gentle bubbles breaking occasionally.)

7 Transfer the lobster tails from the bag to a cutting board or plate that can catch any escaping liquid. Use a fork to remove the meat from the shell and then slice the meat into bite-size pieces and set aside. (If the lobster meat doesn't come out easily, use a chef's knife to split the tail lengthwise, and

then use a fork to scrape the meat from the shell.) Pour any escaped liquid into the skillet with the cream.

8 Drain the pasta, reserving about ½ cup pasta water. Add the pasta to the skillet and toss it gently with the cream to combine. Add the lobster meat and the juice of 1 lemon. If the sauce is too thick, add a splash of the reserved pasta water to loosen it up.

9 Add the parsley and basil to the pasta, turn the heat off, and toss well to combine. Serve the pasta hot with a generous squeeze of lemon.

Spaghetti with Butter-Poached Lobster Tails will keep, in an airtight container in the refrigerator, for 1 day.

NOTE Frozen lobster tails often have ice clinging to them, which will water down the sauce. Rinsing them helps them shed the ice. Use a cloth rather than paper towels to dry them; paper towels may stick to the damp, frozen lobster.

CHAPTER 7

Eggs

To the long list of eggs' virtues—nutrition, versatility, flavor—we can add one that has only recently surfaced: They come encased in their own sous vide packaging.

SOUS VIDE SMARTER:

PAMPER YOUR EGGS

As forgiving as cooking sous vide usually is, eggs present a special case: Overshoot a little or undercook a bit and you may end up with a different result. So, while leaving a piece of beef to cook sous vide for an extra 15 minutes probably won't bring different results, that extra time might change the texture of the egg. (It would still be edible! It just might not be the consistency you bargained for.)

Because eggs take one factor out of sous vide cooking—no messing around with bags or jars—and because they're inexpensive, they're a good low-stakes starting point for getting the feel of sous vide cooking.

One caveat: Take seriously the caution in the instructions to lower the eggs into the water with a slotted spoon, as tempting as it might be to just drop them in. If an egg cracks, it's not the end of the world. It's even possible that the membrane that lines the inside of the shell will stay intact and keep the egg inside. Either way, if you need to give your circulator a little TLC after an incident, see the FAQ for "How do I clean my sous vide circulator?" (page 20).

Perfectly Poached Eggs

TOTAL TIME: 30 minutes   **ACTIVE TIME:** 5 minutes   **YIELD:** 8 eggs

A well-poached egg is a beautiful thing, with a thickened but soft yolk and a white that's set to perfection, short of hard-cooked but not running away. Consider poached eggs with breakfast, lunch, or dinner. Try one on a piece of toast, the yolk settling into the crumb of the bread. Serve one atop a salad, the yolk adding its own richness to whatever dressing you choose. Or make it dinner by serving it atop rice with stir-fried vegetables on the side.

8 large eggs

1 Set the water temperature to 167°F. When the water reaches temperature, use a slotted spoon to gently place the eggs in the water.

2 Make a lid out of aluminum foil for your container, leaving a little space for the sous vide circulator. Be sure the water level is high enough to withstand some evaporation and check the water every so often to make sure it stays above the water line.

3 While the eggs cook, fill a medium-size bowl with ice water. Leave enough room so that the eggs will fit without the bowl overflowing.

4 After 12 minutes, use the slotted spoon to remove the eggs from the sous vide bath and place them in the bowl with the ice water.

5 Let the eggs chill for about 1 minute, then remove from the ice bath. Peel and serve immediately.

Perfectly Poached Eggs are best used the same day but will keep overnight in the refrigerator (they should be stored shelled).

TIP
The eggs will leave behind some white when removed from their shells. Eggs closer to their "best by" date will leave behind less white.

Perfect Ramen Eggs

The ideal ramen egg is soft-boiled, with a relatively firm, custardy white and a jammy yolk. With sous vide, that's easy to achieve: Set the water temperature to 165°F and cook for 15 minutes, followed by an ice bath for 3 minutes to cool, before serving warm.

Egg-Topped Pizza
(page 161)

Miso Rice Bowls with Roasted Cauliflower and Poached Eggs

TOTAL TIME: 1 hour   **ACTIVE TIME:** 20 minutes   **YIELD:** Serves 4

This dish has a lot going for it nutritionally. But it doesn't make you choose between nutritional virtue and flavor. The whole grain rice contributes a nuttiness (and fiber), roasted cauliflower lends its combination of soft and crispy bits (and nutrients), miso paste provides umami (and probiotics), while a poached egg gives it all a luscious, rich finish (and protein).

1½ cups long-grain brown rice

3 cups reduced-sodium chicken broth

1 medium-size head cauliflower (about 2½ pounds), trimmed, cored, and broken into florets (about 8 cups)

2 oil-packed anchovies, very finely chopped

⅓ cup extra-virgin olive oil, plus more for serving

2 teaspoons miso paste

8 large eggs

Crushed unsalted pistachios, for serving

1 Set the water temperature to 167°F. Preheat the oven to 450°F.

2 In a fine-mesh sieve, rinse the rice in running water until the water runs clear. Combine the rice and chicken broth in a medium-size saucepan and bring to a boil over medium-high heat. Reduce the heat to medium-low and cook, covered, until the liquid has been absorbed, about

40 minutes. Remove from the heat and stir to fluff. Leave the lid on slightly ajar to keep the rice warm.

3 Meanwhile, prepare the cauliflower: Line a large baking sheet with parchment paper. Place the cauliflower in a large bowl. Toss with the anchovies. In a small bowl, stir together the olive oil and miso paste. (It's okay if the miso doesn't dissolve

completely; it's enough to break it into smaller pieces and soften it.) Pour over the cauliflower and toss to coat. Spread in a single layer on the prepared baking sheet, pouring any remaining olive oil over the cauliflower. Roast for 40 minutes, stirring halfway through, until the cauliflower is quite dark brown and even blackened in some places.

4 Meanwhile, prepare the eggs according to Perfectly Poached Eggs (page 156).

5 In a large bowl, combine the rice and cauliflower. Gently stir to combine. Divide among four shallow serving bowls. Top each with two of the poached eggs. Sprinkle with the pistachios and drizzle with olive oil.

TIP

Take this recipe in a different delicious direction: In Step 5, instead of pistachios and olive oil, use sesame seeds and pistachio oil or ground peanuts and toasted sesame oil.

Upgraded Instant Ramen

TOTAL TIME: 5 minutes   **ACTIVE TIME:** 5 minutes   **YIELD:** Serves 1

Using packaged instant ramen as a starting point rather than a destination opens up a world of possibilities. Here is my biggest ramen hack: Use your taste buds. Yes, there is more to this recipe than that. But it all starts there. Start with half the seasoning packet (already *loaded* with sodium and other flavoring) and taste before continuing. From there, you can build more interesting, fresher flavors than those that came in the packet.

---

1 package (3 ounces) instant ramen, any flavor (see Notes)

2 scallions, very thinly sliced, white and green parts separated

1 large handful baby spinach

½ sheet toasted nori, cut with scissors into small bite-size pieces

½ teaspoon finely grated fresh ginger, plus more to taste

1 teaspoon toasted sesame oil

2 Perfect Ramen Eggs (page 156)

---

1 Prepare the ramen according to the package directions. When the water starts to boil, add the whites of the scallions.

2 When the broth is just off the heat, add the greens of the scallions, spinach, and nori. Stir the broth to wilt the spinach. Stir in half of the seasoning packet and the finely grated ginger. Drizzle the noodles with the sesame oil. Season to taste with a little bit more of the seasoning packet and ginger, if desired. Top with Perfect Ramen Eggs. Serve hot.

NOTES This is the time to get creative. While the closest supermarket may offer only a handful of varieties of ramen, searching a bit farther afield can yield a better or different selection. So can spending a little more. While instant ramen can be *cheap*, spending even a dollar more per packet can improve the variety and taste available. Also, would it surprise you to learn that searching the internet for "instant ramen reviews" will bring you more than a lifetime of reading? Don't say I didn't warn you.

Some varieties of instant ramen have both dry and liquid seasoning; if that's the case, add half of each.

6 IDEAS FOR SOUS VIDE EGGS

Open-Face Smoked Salmon Sandwiches

For each sandwich, toast a large piece of hearty country-style bread. Rub a clove of garlic over the bread and place 1 ounce of smoked salmon on top. Top with *chopped hard-cooked egg* (page 163) or *warmed poached egg* (page 156). Finish with a dash of freshly ground black pepper.

Salted Baby Potatoes

Place 1½ pounds of baby potatoes in a large pot and add water to just cover. Add 1 tablespoon of table salt. Bring the water to a boil over high heat and then simmer over medium heat until a sharp knife easily pierces a potato's skin, about 15 minutes. Pour off the water. Return the pot with the potatoes to the stove over low heat, letting any remaining water evaporate, 1 minute. Serve with ketchup or malt vinegar alongside *sliced hard-cooked eggs* (page 163) or *warmed poached eggs* (page 156) topped with freshly ground black pepper.

Sautéed Mushrooms

In a large skillet over medium-high heat, melt 2 tablespoons unsalted butter. Add 2 pounds sliced white mushrooms and sprinkle with ½ teaspoon each table salt and freshly ground black pepper. Sauté mushrooms until golden and tender. Top with crumbled goat cheese and chopped chives. Serve with *sliced hard-cooked eggs* (page 163) or *warmed poached eggs* (page 156), topped with coarse salt and freshly ground black pepper.

Deviled Eggs

Peel 6 cooled *hard-cooked eggs* (page 163) and split lengthwise in half. Remove the yolks and place them in a medium-size bowl. Use a fork to mash the yolks with 3 tablespoons mayonnaise, 1½ teaspoons Dijon mustard, a pinch of table salt, and a pinch of cayenne pepper. Taste and add more salt and cayenne pepper, if desired. Spoon the filling into the whites and garnish with finely chopped chives or flat-leaf parsley before serving.

Egg-Topped Pizza

When a pizza is done, sprinkle chopped *hard-cooked eggs* (page 163) over top. Or crack *poached eggs* (page 156) over the pizza and use a spatula to spread some of the runny yolk.

Caesar Salad Dressing

In a tightly covered jar or container, shake or use a fork to combine 2 *pasteurized eggs* (page 167) with 6 tablespoons extra-virgin olive oil, 2 tablespoons freshly squeezed lemon juice, dash of Worcestershire sauce, 1 teaspoon freshly ground black pepper, a pinch of table salt, and 2 oil-packed anchovies (drained and minced). If the dressing separates, use a fork to beat vigorously or shake again to combine.

No-Fuss Hard-Cooked Eggs

TOTAL TIME: 55 minutes **ACTIVE TIME:** 5 minutes **YIELD:** 6 eggs

Cooking eggs sous vide allows you to replicate results reliably and without fuss. Here, this recipe renders shells that are easy to peel, whites that are picture-perfect, and yolks that are firm and evenly colored. The chickens probably never thought about this when they laid the eggs, but the shells are their own sous vide vessel—no need to bag them. While the recipe calls for six eggs, you are limited only by the size of the vessel. Go ahead and cook a dozen if you want.

6 large eggs

1 Set the water temperature to 194°F. When the water reaches temperature, use a slotted spoon to gently place the eggs in the water.

2 Make a lid out of aluminum foil for your container, leaving a little space for the sous vide circulator. Be sure the water level is high enough to withstand some evaporation and check the water every so often to make sure it stays above the minimum water line.

3 While the eggs cook, fill a medium-size bowl with ice water. Leave enough room so the eggs will fit without the bowl overflowing.

4 After 20 minutes, use the slotted spoon to remove the eggs from the sous vide bath and place them in the bowl with the ice water.

5 When the eggs are chilled, about 15 minutes, remove the eggs. Peel and serve immediately or leave the shells intact and refrigerate for later.

No-Fuss Hard-Cooked Eggs will keep in the refrigerator for up to 1 week.

Sous Vide Egg Bites

TOTAL TIME: 1 hour 20 minutes   **ACTIVE TIME:** 10 minutes   **YIELD:** 6 egg bites

You know something is mainstream when it shows up at the local outpost of an international coffee juggernaut. And for a lot of people, the first they heard of sous vide cooking may have been while they picked out something to eat with their morning coffee. Although these egg bites may be the star of many a morning menu, there's no reason to pay big bucks for them. The eggs come out light and fluffy—almost custardlike—after being whipped together in a blender and then gently cooked at a constant temperature.

---

6 large eggs

½ cup grated sharp cheddar cheese

¼ cup cream cheese, room temperature

¼ teaspoon table salt

¼ teaspoon freshly ground black pepper

⅓ cup cooked ham, small dice

Finely chopped chives, for garnish

---

1 Set the water temperature to 172°F. In a blender or food processor (see Note), combine the eggs, cheddar cheese, cream cheese, salt, and pepper. Blend until smooth, about 20 seconds. Place a scant 1 tablespoon of the ham in each of six 4-ounce canning jars with lids. Divide the egg mixture evenly among the jars (see Tip), leaving about ¾ inch of headspace at the top of each jar. Attach the canning lids and bands to the jars and make the bands fingertip tight (see Glass Jars, page 14).

2 When the water reaches temperature, use canning tongs to gently lower the jars into the water. After 1 hour, remove the jars and place on a towel. Let the jars cool for 10 minutes. (You might hear the lids popping as they cool; this is normal.)

3 Serve straight from the jar, garnished with chives. Or, cool in a bath of half ice and half water for 30 minutes before storing in the refrigerator for up to 5 days.

Sous Vide Egg Bites will keep, in an airtight container in the refrigerator, for up to five days.

4 To reheat, remove the lid and microwave on high for 20 seconds. Let stand for 1 minute, then microwave for an additional 15 seconds. Alternatively, reheat the covered jars in a sous vide bath at 140°F for 15 minutes.

NOTE While blenders and food processors work equally well to mix the ingredients, blenders have the edge when it comes to pouring the eggs into the jars.

TIP
To fill the jars evenly, fill each jar roughly three-quarters full. Eyeball the remaining batter and distribute it equally among the jars, dribbling a little more here and a little less there to even out the distribution.

Sous Vide Egg White Bites

In Step 1, substitute 12 large egg whites for the 6 eggs. (Look for cartons of egg whites in your grocer's refrigerated case and consult the label for the equivalent measurement of 1 egg white.) In Step 1, substitute 1 scant tablespoon of chopped jarred roasted red peppers (leaving behind as much liquid as possible) for the ham. Serve garnished with finely chopped roasted red peppers, chives, and freshly ground black pepper.

Egg Salad

TOTAL TIME: 10 minutes   **ACTIVE TIME:** 10 minutes   **YIELD:** 4 sandwiches

Such a simple dish with such humble ingredients adds up to a rich, tasty lunch or dinner without a lot of hassle. Toasting the buns with butter adds such a lovely grace note, adding richness and crunch to the bread that contrasts with the soft egg salad inside.

2 tablespoons salted butter

4 hot dog buns

¼ cup Homemade Lemony Mayonnaise (page 169) or store-bought mayonnaise

1 stalk celery, trimmed and finely chopped

Large bunch of fresh dill, large stems removed, chopped

2 teaspoons yellow mustard

2 teaspoons fresh lemon juice (if using store-bought mayonnaise)

¼ teaspoon table salt, plus more to taste

¼ teaspoon freshly ground black pepper, plus more to taste

6 No-Fuss Hard-Cooked Eggs (page 163), peeled and coarsely chopped

1 In a skillet large enough to accommodate two hot dog buns, melt half of the butter over medium heat, about 2 minutes. Open two of the buns to expose the soft inside and place them in the pan. Press them down gently to make contact with the skillet. Toast the buns until golden brown, about 3 minutes. Repeat steps with the remaining butter and buns. Set aside.

2 In a medium-size bowl, stir together the mayonnaise, celery, dill (reserve some for garnish), mustard, lemon juice (if using store-bought mayonnaise), salt, and pepper. Add the eggs to the bowl and use a spatula to gently distribute them evenly. Season to taste with salt and pepper.

3 Pile the egg salad into the buns and garnish with fresh dill.

Egg Salad is best served immediately after preparing but will keep, in an airtight container in the refrigerator, for up to 2 days.

3 Riffs on Egg Salad

Use just a pinch of salt and replace the dill with 3 strips of crisp-cooked bacon (see page 62), finely chopped.

Use just a pinch of salt and replace the dill with 2 tablespoons of capers, finely chopped.

Replace the celery with 3 trimmed radishes, finely chopped.

Pasteurized Eggs

TOTAL TIME: 1 hour 30 minutes   **ACTIVE TIME:** 5 minutes   **YIELD:** 6 eggs

If recipes containing raw eggs squick you out for food-safety reasons, good news: You can pasteurize eggs in the shell with your sous vide setup. Raw eggs are not dangerous in themselves but can occasionally harbor dangerous bacteria. Substituting pasteurized eggs for raw can be the way to go.

Follow the directions for No-Fuss Hard-Cooked Eggs (page 163), with these exceptions: Set the temperature to 135°F and cook for 1 hour 15 minutes. Use right away or chill in an ice bath until cool, about 15 minutes, and then refrigerate up to 2 weeks. Mark the eggs to distinguish them from raw ("P" for pasteurized does nicely).

NOTES The eggs can be used as raw eggs, but the whites will be slightly cloudy. This is normal.

Take care when separating the whites and yolks; the yolks in pasteurized eggs may become more fragile and hold together less firmly than in unpasteurized eggs.

Homemade Lemony Mayonnaise

TOTAL TIME: 10 minutes   **ACTIVE TIME:** 10 minutes   **YIELD:** About 1 cup

All cooking is science, but few things highlight this so clearly as making mayonnaise. The lecithin in the egg yolk enables the otherwise impossible: combining oil and water. In this case, that "water" is lemon juice for a nice, fresh zip. Using a pasteurized egg yolk means you don't have any worries about raw egg. Mayonnaise is great on sandwiches, but it also makes a wonderful accompaniment to fish, chicken, beef, eggs, and vegetables. This version is delicious as is but—as you'll see from the variations—also forms a beautiful base to which other flavors can be added.

1 yolk from 1 Pasteurized Egg (page 167),
  room temperature

2 tablespoons fresh lemon juice, from 1 large
  lemon or 2 small lemons (see Notes)

¼ teaspoon table salt, plus more to taste

¼ teaspoon freshly ground black pepper,
  plus more to taste

Dash of cayenne pepper

1 cup neutral vegetable oil, such as corn
  or canola (see Notes)

1 Combine the egg yolk, lemon juice, salt, pepper, and cayenne in a medium-size bowl with high sides. (This helps avoid splashes as you whisk.) Place a kitchen towel under the bowl to steady it while you whisk the mayonnaise. Begin adding the oil, about 1 teaspoon at a time, while beating vigorously with a wire whisk until the mayonnaise starts to thicken.

2 As it thickens, you can add oil more quickly, beating in the remaining oil about 1 tablespoon at a time.

3 Season to taste with salt and pepper. Use immediately or refrigerate. The mayonnaise will thicken as it cools in the refrigerator.

Homemade Lemony Mayonnaise will keep, in an airtight container in the refrigerator, for up to 1 week.

NOTES Avoid bottled juice, which can contribute an off or flat flavor. If you don't have fresh lemons, substitute 1 tablespoon of white wine vinegar and 1 tablespoon water.

Resist any temptation to swap the neutral oil for extra-virgin olive oil, which will overpower the mayonnaise. At most, swap out 1/4 cup of the neutral oil for extra-virgin olive oil and adjust from there for future batches.

TIP

To make this in a food processor or blender: In Step 1, start by adding 1/4 cup of the oil. With the machine running, add the rest of the oil in a very thin stream. (If the mayonnaise becomes too thick, add water, 1 drop at a time, with the machine running until desired consistency is achieved.)

Homemade Mayonnaise Riffs

Your freshly made mayo is perfectly wonderful as is, but it can also be flavored in a number of ways:

LIVEN IT UP WITH LEMON ZEST: Before squeezing the lemons, zest them and fold the zest into the finished mayonnaise.

ADD A TOUCH OF SMOKE: Omit the cayenne pepper and fold 1 tablespoon adobo sauce (from canned chipotles in adobo) into the finished mayonnaise.

STIR IN SOME SCALLIONS: Stir in 1/2 cup finely chopped scallions.

HIT THE SPICE CABINET: Add chili powder, curry powder, paprika, lemon pepper, dried dill, or your favorite spice blend. Use about 1 teaspoon per cup of mayonnaise, but start by adding just a dash to 2 tablespoons of mayonnaise before proceeding with the full batch. Taste and adjust as necessary.

Crispy Cauliflower Spaghetti Carbonara

TOTAL TIME: 1 hour   **ACTIVE TIME:** 20 minutes   **YIELD:** Serves 4

This dish gets its salty, umami punch not from cured pork but from cauliflower tossed with a generous glug of olive oil and a tiny bit of roasted anchovy. The salty cauliflower becomes toasty and crunchy in the oven. For creaminess and tang, pasteurized egg yolks are mixed with freshly grated Parmesan. A sprinkling of toasted and chopped pistachios adds crunch and color. Voilà, a carbonara-inspired meal that has full, rich flavor without pork.

1 large head cauliflower, trimmed, cored and cut into bite-size florets

2 oil-packed anchovy filets, finely chopped

¼ cup extra-virgin olive oil, plus 2 tablespoons

¾ teaspoon table salt

¼ cup shelled raw pistachios (see Notes)

1 pound spaghetti

6 yolks from Pasteurized Eggs (page 167)

1 cup fresh and finely grated Parmesan cheese, plus more for serving (see Notes)

2 teaspoons freshly ground black pepper, plus more to taste

¼ cup chopped fresh dill or flat-leaf parsley (optional)

1 Preheat the oven to 450°F.

2 In a large bowl, combine the cauliflower, anchovies, ¼ cup olive oil, and salt. Toss to combine and transfer to a large rimmed baking sheet. (The cauliflower needs room to breathe to achieve maximum crispiness. Use another baking sheet if it needs more room.) Roast until the cauliflower is deeply browned in spots, about 35 minutes, stirring once halfway through.

3 Meanwhile, place the pistachios in a small skillet over medium heat, tossing frequently until they just start to toast and become fragrant, about 5 minutes. (If you're not sure, it's better to err on the side of under-toasted.) Coarsely chop the pistachios and set aside.

4 Bring a large pot of generously salted water to a boil over high heat. Break the spaghetti in half, and cook according to the package directions. (Check the pasta 3 minutes before the package directions indicate. It's al dente when biting into a strand reveals a very tiny core of uncooked pasta. This is what provides the bite and bounce to well-cooked pasta. Stop cooking it immediately.) Drain the pasta, reserving about 1 cup of the pasta water.

5 In a large bowl, whisk the egg yolks, 1 cup Parmesan, 2 teaspoons pepper, and 2 tablespoons olive oil until thick. Add the pasta and ½ cup of the pasta water and toss vigorously to create a creamy sauce that coats the pasta, about 1 minute. Add more pasta water, 1 tablespoon at a time, if sauce is too thick to evenly coat the pasta. (You will probably need that extra water, but don't add it at the start. Wait to see how it's shaping up first.) Add the cauliflower and dill, if using, and toss to distribute. Season to taste with salt and pepper. Divide pasta among four bowls. Top with the pistachios and Parmesan cheese. Serve hot.

Crispy Cauliflower Carbonara Spaghetti will keep, in an airtight container in the refrigerator, for up to 3 days. Reheat in a skillet over medium heat with a splash of hot water, stirring occasionally, until warm.

NOTES If you can't find raw pistachios, feel free to use roasted, unsalted shelled pistachios instead.

This is about 1 ounce of Parmesan. Freshly and finely grated Parmesan cheese has a fluffy, snowlike texture that means 1 cup is not as much cheese as yielded by other kinds of grating. If you're measuring by volume and not weight, start with ½ cup of cheese, taste and work up from there.

TIPS

For easier cleanup, line the baking sheet with parchment paper before roasting the cauliflower. Allow an extra 5 minutes for the cauliflower to become deeply browned.

To warm the pasta bowls, put the pasta water to good use: After reserving the 1 cup of water for the sauce, divide the remaining water among the bowls. Pour out the water just before adding the pasta to serve.

This is a great time to use whole wheat pasta. Substitute an equal amount of your favorite shape for the spaghetti.

CHAPTER 8

Vegetables

The precise temperature control that sous vide cooking offers allows you to extract maximum flavor from vegetables without the risk of overcooking them. The technique produces vegetables with a gently yielding crunch, a unique texture that's difficult to achieve through any other cooking method.

ACHIEVE VEGETABLE PERFECTION

Cooking vegetables sous vide presents special challenges— and special rewards.

The rewards first: Precision cooking means just that—vegetables are neither overdone nor underdone, every time. It's a good way to honor and celebrate the produce. Cooking vegetables sous vide means bringing out the best in each vegetable, the flavors and texture unique to each.

Now, did I say something about challenges? There are challenges. One of them is the hotter water. Universally, vegetables cook at much higher temperatures than meats. (This might run counter to your initial thoughts about vegetables being more delicate than meat, but it has to do with temperatures being high enough to break down cell walls.) This hotter water—temperatures approaching a soft simmer—means that popping your hands into the water will cause pain and possibly injury. The things you can manage with 132°F water are downright dangerous with 185°F water. Respect that temperature and don't take a chance with burning yourself. Make sure, too, that your vessel is somewhere that won't be damaged by that heat.

Because sous vide cooking vegetables requires higher temperatures, it can be particu-larly handy to heat the water on the stovetop to get started, rather than waiting for the circulator to bring it up to temp. Covering the pot with aluminum foil helps retain the heat and prevent water loss to evaporation.

That hotter water means that any little pockets of air in your bag will expand and, like a hot air balloon, fight to raise the bag to the surface. This means that you may find yourself struggling to keep that sealed bag submerged in scalding hot water. These tips are best used in combination:

Choose the right bag: Use vacuum-sealed polyethylene. This will sometimes mean enough air is removed to avoid the other steps being necessary. Alternatively, you can use a reusable silicone bag. These stand up well to the heat but make removing all of the air more difficult. Avoid zip-top freezer bags, which can't stand up to the high heat and will break.

Use weights: Use weights in the bag (see page 15).

Use tongs: Avoid touching the water when grasping and moving the bag.

Use a ramekin: Place the ramekin in the water, let it fill with water, and let it submerge the bag with its weight. Remember to use the tongs to move the ramekin.

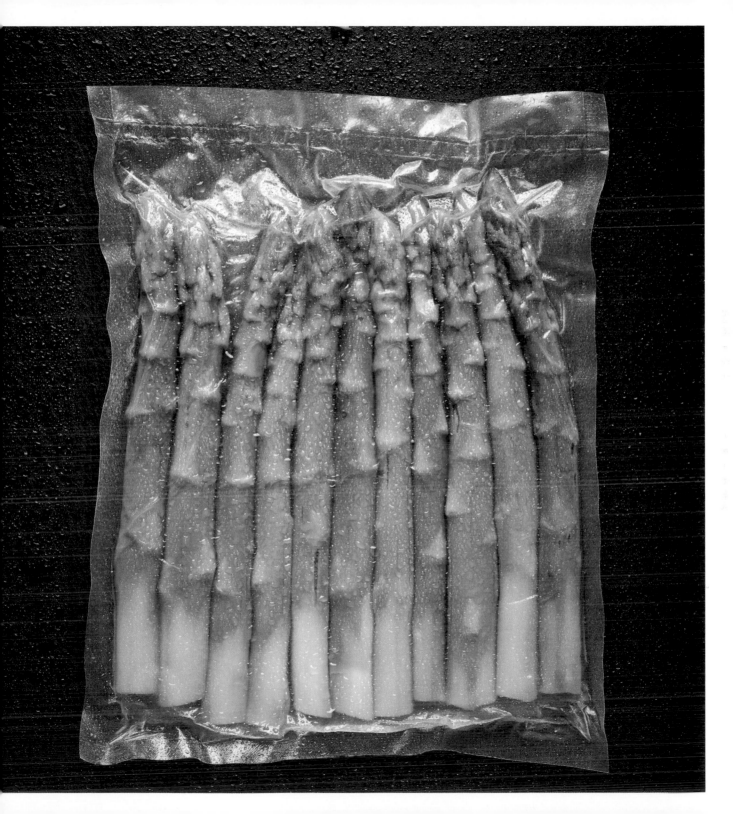

Simple Sous Vide Carrots

TOTAL TIME: 1 hour 20 minutes   **ACTIVE TIME:** 10 minutes   **YIELD:** Serves 3

How to make carrots more . . . carrot-y? Sous vide. After the soak, the carrots emerge softened but not soft, with plenty of tasty juices to form a sauce. Sautéing briefly sets the carrots up, with a deep, rich, standout flavor, for a starring role at any meal. For a more vibrantly colored dish with the same great flavor, look for carrots in hues of orange, yellow, and purple, sometimes available from farmers markets or specialty stores.

---

1 pound young carrots (the freshest you can find), trimmed and peeled (see Notes)

2 tablespoons salted butter, cut into small chunks

Finely chopped chives, for garnish

---

1 Set the water temperature to 185°F. Place the carrots and butter in the bag, making sure that the carrots don't overlap and that the butter is evenly distributed. Seal the bag.

2 When the water reaches temperature, place the bagged carrots in the water. After 1 hour, remove the bagged carrots from the water. Pour the carrots and juices into a large sauté pan over medium-high heat. Cook, stirring frequently and tossing the carrots in liquid, until it thickens slightly and forms a sauce, about 2 minutes.

3 Transfer carrots to a serving dish. Pour the sauce over and garnish with the chives. Serve hot.

Simple Sous Vide Carrots will keep, in an airtight container in the refrigerator, for up to 1 week.

NOTES Choose carrots no thicker than your thumb. If you have thicker carrots, chop them into 2-inch chunks and cut in half lengthwise if necessary to create pieces that are about the circumference of a thumb. In a pinch, "baby-cut carrots" will work.

About 1¼ pounds of young carrots with the greens attached will yield about 1 pound of trimmed carrots once they are trimmed and peeled.

TIP

Stash the washed and trimmed ends and peels in the freezer for up to 3 months and use as part of making vegetable or chicken broth.

Carrots with Butter and Brandy

In Step 1, add 1 tablespoon brandy and ¼ teaspoon freshly ground pepper to the bag with the carrots. Garnish cooked carrots with flat-leaf parsley instead of chives.

Miso-Butter Carrots

In Step 1, use unsalted butter and add 1 tablespoon red miso to the bag with the carrots. Massage the bag to distribute the miso evenly before cooking.

Perfect Sous Vide Asparagus

TOTAL TIME: 20 minutes   **ACTIVE TIME:** 10 minutes   **YIELD:** Serves 3

The arrival of local asparagus heralds the beginning of the growing season. That makes it worthy of celebration. Cooking asparagus sous vide means no limp stalks and no overly crunchy bites. It's spring on a plate.

1 pound thin asparagus (¼ to ½ inch in diameter)

Table salt

Coarse salt, for serving

Extra-virgin olive oil, for serving

1 Set the water temperature to 185°F. Trim about 1 inch from end of each asparagus stalk. If the bottom of a stalk is woody and tough, use a vegetable peeler to expose the tender core of that part of the stem. Place the asparagus in a single layer in a bag. Add a pinch of table salt and seal the bag.

2 When the water reaches temperature, place the bagged asparagus in the water. After 10 minutes, remove the bagged asparagus from the water. Transfer asparagus to a serving platter.

3 Drizzle with olive oil and sprinkle with coarse salt. Serve hot.

Perfect Sous Vide Asparagus is best served immediately, but will keep, in an airtight container in the refrigerator, for up to 2 days. To reheat, microwave on medium power for 1 to 2 minutes.

Asparagus with Lemon and Extra-Virgin Olive Oil

In Step 1, add half of a seeded and very thinly sliced lemon and 2 tablespoons extra-virgin olive oil to the bag with the asparagus. Discard lemon slices after cooking. To serve, squeeze remaining half of lemon over cooked asparagus. Drizzle with extra-virgin olive oil and sprinkle with coarse salt.

Asparagus with Crisped Pancetta

TOTAL TIME: 10 minutes   **ACTIVE TIME:** 10 minutes   **YIELD:** Serves 4

The tiny cubes of pancetta in this dish provide not only bursts of salinity to complement the fresh, green flavor of the asparagus, but also bits of crispness and that soft, luscious quality that pork fat can provide. The pancetta crisps up in the pan while the asparagus is having its bath; the whole dish doesn't take much longer than the 10 minutes it takes to cook the asparagus.

1 tablespoon extra-virgin olive oil, plus more for serving

2 ounces pancetta, diced

1 recipe Perfect Sous Vide Asparagus (page 179)

Freshly ground black pepper

Freshly grated Parmesan cheese, for serving

1 Heat the olive oil in a large skillet over medium-high heat, about 1 minute. Add the pancetta, reduce heat to medium, and cook the pancetta, stirring frequently, until crispy and it has rendered some of its fat, about 7 minutes.

2 Add the cooked asparagus to the skillet with the pancetta and fat. Cook over medium heat, moving the asparagus around with a spatula constantly, until coated with fat, about 1 minute.

3 Transfer the asparagus and pancetta to a serving platter. Sprinkle with black pepper and Parmesan cheese to taste. Serve warm.

Asparagus with Crisped Pancetta is best served immediately, but will keep, in an airtight container in the refrigerator, for up to 2 days.

Asparagus with Butter and Thyme Sauce

TOTAL TIME: 10 minutes   **ACTIVE TIME:** 10 minutes   **YIELD:** Serves 4

The fresh, green flavor of asparagus takes on another savory dimension when cooked—sous vide, of course—in chicken broth. The dish finishes off with a spin on beurre monté, a classic preparation in which butter is combined with water over low heat while staying emulsified, yielding a creamy, buttery sauce that, here, is flecked with fresh thyme.

PREP NOTE: Prepare Perfect Sous Vide Asparagus with 1/3 cup chicken broth instead of salt.

---

1 recipe Perfect Sous Vide Asparagus (page 179); see Prep Note

5 tablespoons unsalted butter, cut into 10 cubes

1/4 teaspoon freshly ground black pepper

Table salt, to taste

Leaves from 2 sprigs fresh thyme

---

1 Transfer cooked asparagus to a serving platter and cover with aluminum foil to keep warm while you make the sauce.

2 Pour 2 tablespoons of the juices from the bag into a small saucepan over medium-high heat, discarding or refrigerating the rest. Cook until reduced by half, 1 to 2 minutes. (Don't step away; there isn't much liquid, and it will reduce quickly.) Reduce the heat to low. (If the burner is still hot, switch to a different burner.) Add the butter, one piece at a time, whisking constantly to incorporate each piece of butter before adding the next, until all of the butter is incorporated and smooth, about 5 minutes.

3 Season with the black pepper and salt to taste. Stir in the thyme leaves and pour the sauce over the asparagus. Serve warm.

Asparagus with Butter and Thyme Sauce is best served immediately.

TIP

Leftover beurre monté can be stored in a tightly sealed container in the refrigerator and used like butter. While it will not maintain the same consistency as the original sauce, it is delicious on potatoes, fish, and pasta.

Better Buttered Corn on the Cob

TOTAL TIME: 35 minutes   **ACTIVE TIME:** 10 minutes   **YIELD:** Serves 4

Sous vide cooking locks the flavor in the bag, keeping all that corny goodness for you and not the cooking water. While it is possible to sous vide corn with the husks still on, that leaves you with the tricky situation of having to shuck hot cooked corn. Better to deal with the husks beforehand. Another bonus: The butter in the bag contributes its flavor not to the husks that will be discarded, but rather to the kernels that will be savored.

---

4 ears fresh sweet corn, shucked (see Note)	Pinch of table salt
2 tablespoons salted butter, plus more for serving	

---

1 Set the water temperature to 185°F.

2 Place the corn, 2 tablespoons butter, and salt in the bag with sous vide weights or 2 stainless steel spoons (see Weights, page 15). Gently massage the bag to evenly coat. Seal the bag.

3 When the water reaches temperature, place the bagged corn in the water. After 25 minutes, remove the bagged corn from the water. Serve hot with additional butter.

Better Buttered Corn on the Cob will keep, in an airtight container in the refrigerator, for up to 2 days. Cut kernels from the cob and serve chilled.

NOTE Use your microwave to shuck the corn: Cut about 2 inches off each cob from the stalk end, (that's where nature provides the cob's "handle"), leaving the husk intact. Place the corn on a plate and microwave on high for 2 minutes. Use a kitchen towel to carefully grasp a cob by the uncut end. Shake each cob until the shucked corn falls out from the husk and silk. (If any silk remains, remove it.)

Corn on the Cob with Chili and Lime

In Step 2, omit the butter and salt. Add 1 tablespoon chili powder, the zest and juice of 1 lime, and 1 teaspoon sugar to the bag with the corn. Massage bag to evenly coat. Proceed with Step 3.

Corn on the Cob with Curry Powder

In Step 2, add 1 tablespoon mild curry powder to the bag with the corn, butter, and salt. Massage bag to evenly coat. Proceed with Step 3.

Foolproof Sous Vide Beets

TOTAL TIME: 3 hours 45 minutes   **ACTIVE TIME:** 15 minutes   **YIELD:** Serves 3

These perfectly cooked beets are like little red jewels, bursting with an incomparable earthy sweetness. I find it easier to peel beets with a vegetable peeler before they're cooked and the skins become slippery. It also means they won't end up cooking with any dirt clinging to their skins.

1 pound medium beets (2 to 3 inches in diameter), trimmed, peeled, and halved stem to tip

2 tablespoons extra-virgin olive oil, plus more for serving

½ teaspoon table salt, plus more to taste

½ teaspoon freshly ground black pepper, plus more to taste

1 Set the water temperature to 187°F. Make a lid out of aluminum foil for your container, leaving a little space for the sous vide circulator. Place the beets, olive oil, salt, and pepper in the bag with weights (see page 15). Seal the bag.

2 When the water reaches temperature, place the bagged beets in the water. After 3½ hours, remove the bagged beets from the water. Remove the beets from the bag (careful—beet juice stains), discarding the juices and placing the beets on a cutting board. Cut beet halves into wedges and transfer to a serving platter.

3 Drizzle the beets with olive oil and season to taste with salt and pepper. Serve warm.

Foolproof Sous Vide Beets will keep, in an airtight container in the refrigerator, for up to 3 days.

TIP

For a bit of heat, in Step 1, add a small pinch of cayenne pepper to the bag with the beets, oil, salt, and pepper.

Beets with Balsamic Vinegar

In Step 1, reduce the olive oil to 1 tablespoon and add 2 tablespoons balsamic vinegar. In Step 3, drizzle the cooking liquid over the cooked beets. Serve with freshly grated Parmesan cheese.

Beets with Black Pepper and Pistachios

TOTAL TIME: 10 minutes   **ACTIVE TIME:** 10 minutes   **YIELD:** Serves 4

The soft texture and sweet flavor of beets combines well with the nutty crunch of the pistachios, just as the brilliant red hue of the beets and muted green color of the pistachios go together beautifully. A dusting of orange zest and good glug of olive oil round out a stunning side dish.

1 recipe Foolproof Sous Vide Beets (page 187), cooled and halved, juices reserved

¼ cup shelled raw pistachios

1 small orange

Extra-virgin olive oil, for serving

¼ teaspoon coarse salt, plus more to taste

¼ teaspoon coarsely ground black pepper, plus more to taste

1 Place the beets and juices in a serving bowl.

2 Toast the pistachios in a small skillet over medium heat, tossing frequently until they just start to toast and become fragrant, about 5 minutes. (If you're not sure, it's better to err on the side of under-toasted.) Transfer the pistachios to a cutting board and coarsely chop.

3 Zest the orange over the beets, add about half of the pistachios, and toss with the juices. Drizzle with extra-virgin olive oil and sprinkle with the salt and pepper. Sprinkle the remaining pistachios on top. Serve chilled or at room temperature.

Beets with Black Pepper and Pistachios will keep, in an airtight container in the refrigerator, for up to 3 days.

Beets with Greek Yogurt and Dill

TOTAL TIME: 1 hour 15 minutes   **ACTIVE TIME:** 15 minutes   **YIELD:** Serves 4

The natural sweetness of beets is offset by the tang of yogurt and the lively, herbaceous flavor of dill in this brilliantly hued dish. The raw garlic infuses the yogurt with flavor but is removed before serving so no one bites into it. This recipe is best with a generous amount of fresh dill, so ideally you will make it when you have available more than the little plastic clamshell cases of dill at the grocer. A "large bunch" in this case means something resembling a respectably sized head of lettuce and may be most readily available at a farmers market during your local growing season.

½ cup plain Greek yogurt (full fat or 2%)

2 cloves garlic, peeled and split in half lengthwise

1 large bunch fresh dill

Dash of table salt

Dash of freshly ground black pepper

1 recipe Foolproof Sous Vide Beets (page 187), cooled, halved, and sliced ¼ inch thick

1 Stir together the yogurt and garlic in a serving bowl. Let stand for 1 hour.

2 Wash and dry the dill and remove all but the smallest stems, reserving 2 large attractive sprigs for garnish. Strip the remaining smaller dill fronds from the main stem. (See Tip.) Remove the garlic from the yogurt and discard. Stir the salt, pepper, dill fronds, and sliced beets into the yogurt.

3 Garnish with dill sprigs. Serve chilled or at room temperature.

Beets with Greek Yogurt and Dill will keep, in an airtight container in the refrigerator, for up to 3 days.

TIP

To strip the fronds from the main stem: Grab hold of the large stem between your thumb and forefinger, then sweep the two fingers up the stem.

CHAPTER 9

Desserts

While sous vide cooking may have earned its reputation with a savory repertoire, the technique provides a sweeter side to discover, too. Egg-based desserts, whether chilled custards, cheesecakes, or ice creams, lend themselves particularly well to the precise temperature control of sous vide. You'll also find that this method can elevate something as simple as whole fruit.

"Baked" Pears with Vanilla Bean   Salted Dulce de Leche

Berry Cheesecake   Pumpkin Pie Cups

Silky Lemon Curd   Sous Vide Crème Brûlée

Apples with Pie Spices   Shortcut "Cold Brew" Coffee

Peppered Potato Chip Ice Cream

"Baked" Pears with Vanilla Bean

TOTAL TIME: 1 hour 5 minutes   **ACTIVE TIME:** 5 minutes   **YIELD:** Serves 4

Pears cooked sous vide take on an almost silky texture and deliciously pure pear flavor. Like a lot of things cooked sous vide, the flavor of the pear concentrates and intensifies. The pear becomes pear-ier. Here, nothing hides that flavor. Spices and just a smidge of sugar play important supporting roles, while the vanilla ice cream complements and highlights the deep flavor of the pear.

---

4 Bosc pears, peeled

2 tablespoons sugar

1 cinnamon stick, about 4 inches

4 whole cloves

Pinch of freshly grated nutmeg

Dash of table salt

1 whole vanilla bean

Vanilla ice cream, for serving

---

1 Set the water temperature to 175°F.

2 Place the pears, sugar, cinnamon stick, cloves, nutmeg, and salt in the bag. Using a small sharp knife, split the vanilla bean lengthwise and scrape the vanilla seeds into the bag. Seal the bag.

3 When the water reaches temperature, place the bagged pears in the water. After 1 hour, remove the bagged pears from the water. Open the bag and pour out the juices into a ramekin. Gently remove the pears from the bag and place them on a cutting board. Slice the pears, leaving behind the cores and stems.

4 Serve warm with vanilla ice cream, spooning the pear juice from the ramekin over the pears and ice cream.

"Baked" Pears with Vanilla Bean will keep, in an airtight container in the refrigerator, for up to 3 days.

Berry Cheesecake

TOTAL TIME: 1 hour 30 minutes, plus 5 hours of cooling   **ACTIVE TIME:** 30 minutes   **YIELD:** Serves 4

If I told you that this was the world's best and easiest cheesecake, my only concern with the hyperbole would be that it might somehow fall short. It's that good. And it's that easy, a great make-ahead dessert for a special occasion or no occasion at all. Be sure to check out the Variations for ways to riff on perfection.

CHEESECAKE:

1 package (8 ounces) cream cheese, room temperature

¼ cup sugar

1 large egg

⅓ cup heavy cream

½ teaspoon pure vanilla extract

Finely grated zest of 1 small lemon

Pinch of table salt

TOPPING:

1 cup fresh or frozen blueberries, blackberries, or raspberries, or a combination (see Notes)

1½ teaspoons sugar

½ teaspoon lemon juice

Pinch of table salt

¼ cup chocolate cookie crumbs (see Notes)

1 Set the water temperature to 176°F.

2 In a large bowl, beat the cream cheese and sugar with a hand mixer on medium speed until light and fluffy, about 1 minute 30 seconds. Add the egg and beat until just combined, about 20 seconds. Slowly add the cream while mixing at low speed until fully incorporated. Add the vanilla, lemon zest, and salt and continue to mix until combined, about 10 seconds, scraping down the sides of the bowl with a spatula.

3 Transfer the batter to a large measuring cup or a bowl with a spout. Divide among four 4-ounce canning jars. (See Notes and Tip.) There should be about ½ inch of room at the top of each jar. Use a damp paper towel to wipe the rims clean of batter. Attach the canning lids and bands to the jars and make the bands fingertip tight (see Glass Jars, page 14).

4 When the water reaches temperature, use canning tongs to gently lower the jars into the water. After 1 hour, remove the jars. Let the cheesecakes cool at room temperature until just warm, about 1 hour. (You may hear the lids popping as they cool; this is normal.) Refrigerate the jars and chill at least 4 hours.

5 About 15 minutes before you're ready to serve, make the topping: In a small saucepan over low heat, combine the berries, sugar, lemon juice, and salt. Cook until the berries soften slightly but still hold together, about 2 minutes. Remove topping from the heat and allow to cool to room temperature, about 15 minutes.

6 Top each cheesecake with about 1 tablespoon of cookie crumbs and a spoonful of topping.

Berry Cheesecake will keep, in an airtight container in the refrigerator, for up to 5 days.

NOTES Chocolate cookie crumbs are a thing. Look for them in the baking aisle. This is to say that you don't have to buy chocolate sandwich cookies and eat the middles and crush the chocolate cookie part yourself. I mean, you can. But you don't have to.

Double-check your jar size: 4-ounce jars are small and squat (about 2 inches tall).

This is a great place to use frozen berries. Keep the quantities the same, but start the heat at medium and stir frequently until the berries thaw, about 3 minutes, then turn the heat to low and continue as above.

TIP
To fill the jars evenly, fill each jar roughly three-quarters full. Eyeball the remaining batter and distribute it equally among the jars, dribbling a little more here and a little less there to even out the distribution.

Go Vanilla

Omit the lemon zest. In Step 2, add the scraped seeds of 1 split vanilla bean.

Go Chocolate

Omit the lemon zest. In Step 2, beat in 3 tablespoons of cocoa powder with the sugar. Double down on the chocolate by topping each cheesecake with mini chocolate chips. (The berry-and-cookie-crumb route is also delicious here.)

Go Caramel

Omit the lemon zest and top with Dulce de Leche al Café or Vanilla Bean Dulce de Leche (page 204).

Silky Lemon Curd

TOTAL TIME: 1 hour 35 minutes   **ACTIVE TIME:** 5 minutes   **YIELD:** About 1 pint

This lemon curd is good enough to eat from the jar and, honestly, there is almost no reason to go beyond that. Almost. You can also spread it on toast or English muffins, turn it into a tart using a prebaked shell and fresh berries, serve it on pancakes or waffles, stir it into plain yogurt, slather it between cake layers, or use it along with whipped ricotta as a filling for store-bought crepes.

3 medium-size lemons

¾ cup sugar

Pinch of salt

3 large egg yolks, lightly beaten

¼ cup unsalted butter, melted and cooled

1 Set the water temperature to 180°F.

2 With a microplane grater, finely zest the lemons into a small bowl or ramekin. (This should yield about 2 tablespoons of tightly packed zest.) Squeeze the lemon juice into a container and set it aside. (You should have about ½ cup of juice; if not, top it up with juice from another lemon.)

3 In a blender, combine the sugar, lemon zest, and salt. Blend until the mixture is ground into a fine powder, about 1 minute. (If the sugar clumps, turn off and unplug the machine; break up the clumps with a long spoon or spatula and then continue

to blend.) Add the lemon juice, egg yolks, and butter and blend until the mixture is thoroughly blended, 20 to 30 seconds.

4 Divide between two half-pint jars with canning lids (leaving about ½ inch of headspace). Attach the canning lids and bands to the jars and make the bands fingertip tight (see Glass Jars, page 14).

5 When the water reaches temperature, place the jars in the water. After 1 hour, remove the jars. Let lemon curd cool to room temperature, about 30 minutes. If white foam has set at the top of the jars, gently shake to homogenize the curd. (You

may hear the lids popping as the jars cool; this is normal.)

6 Refrigerate the jars. Serve lemon curd chilled or at room temperature.

Silky Lemon Curd will keep, in an airtight container in the refrigerator, for up to 2 weeks or up to 3 months in the freezer.

NOTES Three lemons should yield about 2 tablespoons of zest and 1/2 cup of juice. If you are running a bit short, top each off with zest and/or juice from an additional lemon.

While this lemon curd is cooked in canning jars and while the jars may even seal themselves in the sous vide bath, this is not a shelf-stable product; it must be stored in the refrigerator or freezer.

TIP

Every last dollop counts. Turn any last lemon curd lingering in the jar into a salad dressing by adding about 3 parts extra-virgin olive oil to 1 part lemon curd. Add a pinch each of salt and pepper and shake vigorously. Puckery, savory, lightly sweet, and fresh-tasting—delicious!

Apples with Pie Spices

TOTAL TIME: 1 hour 5 minutes   **ACTIVE TIME:** 5 minutes   **YIELD:** Serves 4

Apple pie is all about the crust, of course, but it is also about the piles of apples layered with spices. Here, those spices soak into the apple, permeating the outer layer with the warm taste of cinnamon and other autumn spices. Stash these apples in the refrigerator and use them as a stir-in for the morning's oatmeal (perhaps with Salted Dulce de Leche, page 204), or serve them with a dollop of thick, full-fat Greek yogurt for a simple make-ahead dessert (that could double as breakfast).

---

4 medium-size Granny Smith apples, peeled but not cored, stems left on if present

1 tablespoon dark brown sugar

1 teaspoon ground cinnamon

½ teaspoon ground cardamom

½ teaspoon allspice

½ teaspoon ground ginger

Pinch of ground nutmeg

2 tablespoons unsalted butter

---

1 Set the water temperature to 175°F.

2 In a medium-size bowl, stir together the brown sugar, cinnamon, cardamom, allspice, ginger, and nutmeg. Roll each apple in the spice mixture to coat. Place the apples, butter, and any remaining spice mixture in the bag. Seal the bag.

3 When the water reaches temperature, place the bagged apples in the water. After 1 hour, remove the bagged apples from the water. Open the bag and pour out the juices into a ramekin. Gently remove the apples from the bag and transfer to a cutting board. Slice the apples, leaving behind the cores and stems.

4 Serve warm, at room temperature, or chilled.

Apples with Pie Spices will keep, in an airtight container in the refrigerator, for up to 5 days.

Peppered Potato Chip Ice Cream

TOTAL TIME: 17 hours   **ACTIVE TIME:** 30 minutes   **YIELD:** 1 quart

Using thick, ridged chips gives you an advantage here: The chips need to stand up to a good, long soak in cream, and the heft of these chips gives them the best chance. When it comes to serving, the chip garnish is not *just* for looks—though it does look cool. It helps clue in people to what they're eating, which is delicious but unexpected. Of course, you can leave off the garnish and see who guesses the flavor first. The flavor might be on the tip of their tongues—literally— but it doesn't quickly leap to mind.

1½ cups whole milk

1½ cups heavy cream

2 ounces thick-cut ridged salt-and-pepper
potato chips, plus more for garnish (see Note)

6 large egg yolks

¾ cup sugar

1 tablespoon honey

---

1 Set the water temperature to 185°F.

2 In a medium-size saucepan, bring the milk and cream just to a simmer. (Small bubbles will form on the surface; that's hot enough.) Remove from the heat, add the potato chips, and stir gently until the chips are covered in milk and cream. Cover the pan and let stand for 1 hour.

3 Pour the milk mixture through a sieve over a medium-size bowl. In a large bowl, whisk the egg yolks, sugar, and honey. Add

the milk mixture and whisk until combined. Pour the ice cream base into a reusable silicone bag. Seal the bag. (Depending on the type of bag and your dexterity, you may find it helpful to pour it into a pitcher first.)

4 When the water reaches temperature, place the bag in the water. After 1 hour, remove the bag. Run it under cold water in the sink until it's just warm to the touch, about 2 minutes, and then chill in the refrigerator overnight. (See Tip.)

5 Pass the chilled base through a sieve over a medium-size bowl. Freeze in an ice cream maker according to the manufacturer's instructions. Once the custard is frozen (usually about 20 minutes, but let your eyes be your guide), transfer to a freezer-safe container and freeze for at least 4 hours. (Without this step, the ice cream is delicious but more along the lines of soft-serve.) Scoop and serve garnished with crushed salt-and-pepper potato chips.

Peppered Potato Chip Ice Cream is best eaten within 1 week.

TIP

Don't skimp on the chilling. This sits overnight to allow the ice cream the best chance at freezing well. Strapped for time?

Refrigerate the custard at least 6 hours and use an instant-read thermometer to verify the custard is 40°F or below before freezing in the ice-cream machine.

NOTE Potato chips are a mess to measure by volume, so this recipe calls for a weight. Don't have a scale? You can eyeball it. If your bag of potato chips is about 8 ounces, use about one-quarter of the bag in Step 1. As for the garnish, that's up to you—sometimes I use a thin salt-and-pepper chip garnish for a more delicately crispy crunch.

Buttered Popcorn Ice Cream

In Step 2, substitute 2 ounces butter-flavored microwave popcorn, prepared per the package directions, for the potato chips. In Step 5, garnish with a few kernels of popped corn.

Salted Dulce de Leche

TOTAL TIME: 13 hours 5 minutes   **ACTIVE TIME:** 5 minutes   **YIELD:** One 8-ounce jar

This sweet and lightly salty sauce makes a terrific topping for ice cream, a great stir-in for plain yogurt, and a delicious breakfast slathered onto a thick piece of brioche. Take note that while this dulce de leche is cooked in a canning jar and while the jar may even seal itself in the sous vide bath, this is not a shelf-stable product; it must be stored in the fridge.

---

1 can (14 ounces) sweetened condensed milk | ½ teaspoon table salt

---

1 Set the water temperature to 185°F.

2 Pour the sweetened condensed milk into a half-pint canning jar with a lid, leaving about ¼ inch of headspace at the top of the jar. (This will likely leave you with an extra tablespoon or two of sweetened condensed milk.) Add the salt and stir with a small spoon to combine. Attach the canning lid and band to the jar and make the band fingertip tight (see Glass Jars, page 14).

3 When the water reaches temperature, use canning tongs to gently add the jar to the water. After 12 hours, remove the jar. Let the dulce de leche cool at room temperature until just warm to the touch, about 1 hour. (You may hear the lid popping as the jar cools; this is normal.) Use or refrigerate.

Salted Dulce de Leche will keep, in an airtight container in the refrigerator, for up to 2 weeks.

Vanilla Bean Dulce de Leche

Eliminate the salt. Add the seeds from 1 split and scraped vanilla bean. When you take the jar out of the water, open it and stir to redistribute the seeds. Replace the lid and continue to cool at room temperature.

Dulce de Leche al Café

In a small bowl or ramekin, microwave 2 tablespoons of whole or 2% milk (do not use sweetened condensed milk; the coffee will not dissolve properly) for 10 seconds, until very warm. Stir 1 teaspoon instant coffee into the warmed milk and stir until completely dissolved. Pour the coffee-flavored milk in the jar, filling the rest with sweetened condensed milk and leaving ¼-inch headspace at the top of the jar. Stir well before placing the lid on the jar and proceeding with Step 3.

Pumpkin Pie Cups with Toasty
Pumpkin Seeds (page 208)

Pumpkin Pie Cups

TOTAL TIME: 1 hour 30 minutes, plus 5 hours of cooling   **ACTIVE TIME:** 30 minutes   **YIELD:** Serves 6

These single-serving pies break the mold—figuratively!—when it comes to form, but not flavor. All the delicious components are there: the perfectly silky pumpkin custard, the gentle autumnal spices, and the graham cracker crust. They've just been rearranged to take advantage of the even, steady cooking of the sous vide circulator.

PIE FILLING:

1 cup canned pumpkin puree

½ cup light or dark brown sugar

1 large egg

⅓ cup heavy cream

⅓ cup whole milk

½ teaspoon ground ginger

½ teaspoon ground cinnamon

Pinch of ground nutmeg

Pinch of ground cloves

Pinch of table salt

CRUMBLE TOPPING:

4 tablespoons salted butter

½ cup graham cracker crumbs (from about 3 graham large crackers, finely crushed)

1 Set the water temperature to 176°F.

2 In the bowl of a stand mixer fitted with the whisk attachment or in a large bowl with a pouring spout, beat the pumpkin puree, brown sugar, and egg on medium speed until smooth, about 30 seconds. Reduce speed to low and slowly add the cream and milk, mixing until fully incorporated. Gently stir in the ginger, cinnamon, nutmeg, cloves, and salt with a spoon until well combined.

3 Divide the batter among six 4-ounce canning jars. There should be about ¾ inch of headspace at the top of each jar. Use a damp paper towel to wipe the rims clean of batter. Attach the canning lids and bands to the jars and make the bands fingertip tight (see Glass Jars, page 14).

4 When the water reaches temperature, use canning tongs to gently lower the jars into the water. After 1 hour, remove the jars. Let the pumpkin pies to cool at room

temperature until just warm, about 1 hour. (You may hear the lids popping as they cool; this is normal.) Chill in the refrigerator for at least 4 hours.

5 About 20 minutes before you're ready to serve, make the topping: In a small skillet over medium heat, melt the butter. Add the graham cracker crumbs and cook, stirring frequently, until toasted, about 5 minutes. Remove from the heat and let cool to room temperature, about 15 minutes. Top each pie with about 1 tablespoon of the toasted crumbs. Serve chilled.

Pumpkin Pie Cups will keep, in an airtight container in the refrigerator, for up to 5 days.

Pumpkin Pie Cups with Toasty Pumpkin Seeds

Omit crumble topping. Melt 1½ tablespoons salted butter in a small skillet over medium heat. Add ¼ cup raw unsalted pumpkin seeds (pepitas) and cook, shaking occasionally, until toasted, about 6 minutes. (The butter will foam as the seeds toast.) Let cool about 5 minutes. Pour off the butter and store in the refrigerator for later use. (It's good on pasta or with squash.) Top each pumpkin pie with a dollop of crème fraîche. Sprinkle with the toasted pumpkin seeds.

Sous Vide Crème Brûlée

TOTAL TIME: 4 hours 30 minutes, including 3 hours for cooling   **ACTIVE TIME:** 30 minutes   **YIELD:** Serves 4

There really is no substitute for a blow torch, which is why you don't see construction workers sticking metal beams under the broiler. And, honestly, you have a sous vide circulator, so we're a little beyond "I don't have room for another gadget!" So, yes, this recipe calls for a culinary blow torch.

---

1 whole vanilla bean

6 large egg yolks

⅓ cup sugar, plus 3 tablespoons for topping

Pinch of table salt

1½ cups heavy cream

---

1 Set the water temperature to 181°F.

2 Using a small sharp knife, split the vanilla bean lengthwise and scrape the seeds into a large bowl with a spout, reserving the pod. Add the egg yolks, the ⅓ cup sugar, and salt, and beat with a hand mixer on medium speed until mixture is smooth and pale yellow in color, about 30 seconds. Add the cream and beat just to combine, about 15 seconds. Add the vanilla bean pod to the custard.

3 Pour the custard into a 1-quart canning jar with a lid. Attach the lid and band to the jar and make the band fingertip tight. (See

Glass Jars, page 14. If the lid will sit above the water line, it's not necessary to be too fussy in terms of tightness here.)

4 When the water reaches temperature, use heat-resistant gloves or canning tongs to place the jar in the water. The water should come up at least above the shoulders of the jar. After 1 hour, use heat-resistant gloves or canning tongs to remove the jar. Let the jar cool at room temperature for about 15 minutes.

5 Use a spatula to scrape any vanilla seeds from the bottom and sides of the jar, and gently stir the custard. Divide among four

4-ounce ramekins, discarding the vanilla bean pod. Firmly tap the bottom of each ramekin against the counter to settle the custard and remove any bubbles. Chill the custards in the refrigerator for 3 hours. (The custards may form a "skin," but since we're taking a blowtorch to them, that's no big deal.)

6 About 45 minutes before you plan to serve, remove the custards from the refrigerator. If there is any moisture pooled on top, gently dab with a paper towel. Place a clean kitchen towel on a baking sheet. Place the ramekins on top. (This protects any fragile surfaces from the flame of the torch.) Sprinkle about 2 teaspoons sugar over each custard, smoothing with the back of a spoon or very gently shaking to distribute evenly. Brush any excess sugar from the sides of the ramekins with a pastry brush or paper towel.

7 Using a kitchen torch (and following the operating instructions that came with it), caramelize the sugar: With the tip of the flame barely kissing the sugar, move the torch back and forth slowly and evenly across the sugar until it is all melted and browned, about 1 minute per custard. (Because you can't un-burn sugar and can always touch up a custard with a quick hit of the flame, it's better to err on the side of under-toasted if you're not sure.) Serve immediately.

Sous Vide Crème Brûlée will keep, covered tightly in plastic wrap in the refrigerator, for up to 3 days. Top with sugar and caramelize right before serving.

Go Lemon

Add a scant ¼ teaspoon lemon extract to the custard in Step 2. In Step 7, sprinkle the finely grated zest of 1 lemon over the toasted sugar.

Go Almond

Add a scant ¼ teaspoon almond extract to the custard in Step 2. In Step 7, sprinkle almond meal or slivered almonds over the toasted sugar. Using a light hand and a low flame, toast the meal or nuts very briefly, perhaps for as little as a few seconds—it happens quickly. If some meal or nuts burn, use a small spoon to remove.

Shortcut "Cold Brew" Coffee

TOTAL TIME: 3 hours, including cooling time   **ACTIVE TIME:** 15 minutes   **YIELD:** About 2½ cups

Cold brew coffee—not to be confused with iced coffee, though cold brew coffee can be iced—typically allows the grounds to sit in the water for 12 to 24 hours at room or refrigerator temperature. It produces a lovely, smooth brew, without any unpleasant bitterness and acidity. This version takes that long process and speeds things up considerably, while still keeping the coffee below typical brewing temperatures. In the winter, I look forward to a hot cup of coffee. In the summer, I long for cold brew coffee served on ice. My friend Emily Wight, a fellow cookbook author, also insists that you try it with tonic water.

⅔ cup plus 2 tablespoons ground coffee, ground for a French press (See Note)

---

1 Set the water temperature to 150°F.

2 In a 1-quart canning jar with a lid, combine coffee and 3½ cups cold water, leaving about 1 inch of headspace at the top. Stir until grounds are thoroughly wet. Attach the lid and band to the jar and make the band fingertip tight. (See Glass Jars, page 14.) If the lid will sit above the water line, it's not necessary to be too fussy in terms of tightness here. But the jars do need to be covered to guard against evaporation.)

3 When water reaches temperature, use heat-resistant gloves or canning tongs to place the jar in the water, which should come up at least above the shoulders of the jar. After 2 hours, use heat-resistant gloves or canning tongs to remove the jar.

4 Filter the coffee: Place a fine-mesh strainer over a large bowl or 1-quart jar. Pour the coffee through the strainer, leaving behind as many grounds as possible in the jar. Depending on the coarseness of your grind and the fineness of your strainer, you may wish to strain the coffee a second time through a paper drip-coffee filter: Dampen a paper filter and line the strainer with it. Filter the coffee again. A little bit of fine sediment may remain; that's okay. It'll sink to the bottom and won't affect flavor.

5 To chill the coffee: Start a new bath with fresh, cold water. Add a generous amount of ice. Set your sous vide circulator to 40°F or its coldest setting. It's not necessary to get the bath down to 40°F—you just want the ice water as cold as possible and you don't want the circulator to heat the water. If the coffee is in a bowl, use a funnel to pour it into a jar. Close the lid and place the jar in the water up to its neck and let cool until it falls below 70°F on an instant-read thermometer, about 30 minutes. (The time and target temperature will vary according to how much ice is used and how cold the water bath is. Colder is better, but don't sweat it if it's not exactly 70°F—as long as it's not still 150°F.) Chill in the refrigerator.

6 Serve over ice or with milk. Dilute with cold water if desired, adding about 2 tablespoons of water at a time and tasting as you go.

Shortcut "Cold Brew" Coffee will keep, in an airtight container in the refrigerator, for up to 2 weeks.

NOTE French press coffee grounds are coarser than the grounds for drip coffee.

TIPS

This cooling technique can also be used for soda, wine, beer, or any sealed beverage.

Don't have 1-quart jars? No problem. The recipe is easy to scale: Use 1/3 cup ground coffee for every 1 1/2 cups water. Be sure to leave about 1 inch of headspace at the top of the jar.

General Sous Vide Times and Temperatures

Cooking preferences and cuts of meat differ—even the same cut may differ depending on the quality, the breed of animal, and how it was raised. That said, sometimes you need a starting place!

The recipes in this book cover a range of foods, but if you need a starting point for your own creations, refer to this chart. Note that thicker pieces will require times toward the longer end of the range.

Beef, steaks
Tender cuts don't generally benefit from longer cooking to break down connective tissue, so the cook times are on the shorter side for sous vide cooking. Choose steaks that are roughly 1 inch thick.

Doneness	Temperature	Time
Rare	132°F	1 hour 30 minutes to 2 hours
Medium-rare	136°F	1 hour 30 minutes to 2 hours
Medium	140°F	1 hour 30 minutes to 3 hours
Medium-well	146°F	1 hour 30 minutes to 2 hours
Well done	152°F	1 hour 30 minutes to 3 hours

Beef, tough cuts (brisket, roasts)
Chewy cuts benefit from longer cooking times to tenderize them. Take care to cut thick pieces of meat (generally, thicker than 2 inches) and bag the pieces in a single layer so they cook safely and evenly.

Doneness	Temperature	Time
Medium	140°F	6 hours to 12 hours
Well done	158°F	5 hours to 10 hours

Pork, chops and tenderloin

Doneness	Temperature	Time
Medium-rare	135°F	1 hour to 3 hours
Medium	145°F	1 hour to 3 hours
Well done	155°F	1 hour to 3 hours

Chicken, white meat

Doneness	Temperature	Time
Tender and moist	150°F	1 hour 30 minutes to 3 hours 30 minutes

Chicken, dark meat

Doneness	Temperature	Time
Juicy and tender	165°F	1 hour 30 minutes to 3 hours 30 minutes

Vegetables		
Doneness	**Temperature**	**Time**
Tender green vegetables	185°F	10 to 20 minutes
Root vegetables	185°F	1 to 2 hours

Fish and seafood

Keep in mind that this yields seafood that, while it may have the texture, appearance, and flavor of being cooked, has not been cooked sufficiently to kill pathogens and must be considered raw for food-safety purposes. This is very important! Some people eat raw seafood and some people do not. Both are reasonable positions, but you should make an informed decision for yourself and should not surprise guests with something they may not have bargained for.

Doneness	Temperature	Time
Opaque throughout	120°F	< 1 hour

Acknowledgments

So many people to thank. Gratitude really expands to occupy the space you allow it.

You know, I kept a daily gratitude journal using an app on my phone. Then the app bit the dust. Three years of gratitude, down the freaking drain!

I did have it backed up, but the backup wouldn't load. I wrote to the developer. And I was very nice because it's difficult to be a jerk when you're complaining about a gratitude journal. But there was nothing they could do.

It's gone, but was I less grateful for the things in that journal? When I was backing up my gratitude journal, what was I saving? Was I preserving that gratitude? No.

The gratitude never went anywhere. And while jotting down notes helped bring the gratitude forward, it was never about the notes. It was about the gratitude. It's all about the gratitude.

Mom, it all goes back to you. Thank you.

Thank you to Christine, to Melanie, to Sarah, to Nick, to Margaret, and to Stu. The years fade into decades, the decades into a lifetime. Did any of us imagine that back in the day? That's how it works and here we are. Still. Thank goodness. Thank *you*.

There is one guy who has eaten *everything* in this book, a lot of it more than once. You might think it would be great to live with a cookbook author. It . . . can be okay. But you should know: There are a lot of dishes. And at some point, it will probably be easier to just do the dishes than to debate whether they were for the book or for lunch or break-fast and where is that line anyway? Bryan never argued, even when I timidly offered, against all odds: "There shouldn't be many dishes!" There were always a lot of dishes. He always did more than his fair share. And that's not even his best quality. Thank you.

To Caroline and to Susan, thanks for listening. Your projects always keep me inspired and striving.

To the intrepid band of recipe testers, I cannot thank you enough. Emily, thank you for saving me—and readers—from myself. That is truly the hardest job of all. Rachel, be careful flagging me down on the street—who knows what I could rope you into next! Lauren, Dana, Mark, Sam, and Lisa: Thank you so much for pitching in.

Megan and Stacey, you weren't so much a part of this book as you were everything leading up to it, and for that I'm very grateful.

To the teams at Chez Nino and Boucherie Lawrence: You provide not just nourishment but inspiration. *Merci.*

Kylie, Sarah, Chloe, Moira, Rebecca, Suzie, and everyone at Workman Publishing: Thank you so much. It's a huge privilege to share with others my passion for food and you make it possible. A big thank-you also to Lisa, Ken, Josh, Cassandra, Saley, and everybody at Waterbury Publications who helped bring this book to life.

Okay. So much gratitude! Wrap it up, Shumski!

Thank you.

Index

Notes

Conversion Tables

APPROXIMATE EQUIVALENTS

I STICK BUTTER = 8 tbs = 4 oz = ½ cup = 115 g

I CUP ALL-PURPOSE PRESIFTED FLOUR = 4.7 oz

I CUP GRANULATED SUGAR = 8 oz = 220 g

I CUP (FIRMLY PACKED) BROWN
SUGAR = 6 oz = 220 g to 230 g

I CUP CONFECTIONERS' SUGAR = 4½ oz = 115 g

I CUP HONEY OR SYRUP = 12 oz

I CUP GRATED CHEESE = 4 oz

I CUP DRIED BEANS = 6 oz

I LARGE EGG = about 2 oz or about 3 tbs

I EGG YOLK = about I tbs

1 EGG WHITE = about 2 tbs

Please note that all conversions are approximate but close enough to be useful when converting from one system to another.

WEIGHT CONVERSIONS

US	METRIC	US	METRIC
½ oz	15 g	7 oz	200 g
1 oz	30 g	8 oz	250 g
1½ oz	45 g	9 oz	275 g
2 oz	60 g	10 oz	300 g
2½ oz	75 g	11 oz	325 g
3 oz	90 g	12 oz	350 g
3½ oz	100 g	13 oz	375 g
4 oz	125 g	14 oz	400 g
5 oz	150 g	15 oz	450 g
6 oz	175 g	1 lb	500 g

LIQUID CONVERSIONS

US	IMPERIAL	METRIC
2 tbs	1 fl oz	30 ml
3 tbs	1½ fl oz	45 ml
¼ cup	2 fl oz	60 ml
⅓ cup	2½ fl oz	75 ml
⅓ cup + 1 tbs	3 fl oz	90 ml
⅓ cup + 2 tbs	3½ fl oz	100 ml
½ cup	4 fl oz	125 ml
⅔ cup	5 fl oz	150 ml
¾ cup	6 fl oz	175 ml
¾ cup + 2 tbs	7 fl oz	200 ml
1 cup	8 fl oz	250 ml
1 cup + 2 tbs	9 fl oz	275 ml
1¼ cups	10 fl oz	300 ml
1⅓ cups	11 fl oz	325 ml
1½ cups	12 fl oz	350 ml
1⅔ cups	13 fl oz	375 ml
1¾ cups	14 fl oz	400 ml
1 cups + 2 tbs	15 fl oz	450 ml
2 cups (1 pint)	16 fl oz	500 ml
2½ cups	20 fl oz (1 pint)	600 ml
3¾ cups	1½ pints	900 ml
4 cups	1¾ pints	1 liter

OVEN TEMPERATURES

°F	GAS MARK	°C	°F	GAS MARK	°C
250	½	120	400	6	200
275	1	140	425	7	220
300	2	150	450	8	230
325	3	160	475	9	240
350	4	180	500	10	260
375	5	190			

Note: Reduce the temperature by 20°C (68°F) for fan-assisted ovens.

About the Author

Daniel Shumski is a writer and editor who has hunted ramen in Tokyo for the *Washington Post* and tracked down ice cream in Buenos Aires for the *Los Angeles Times*. Between stints at the *Chicago Sun-Times* and the *Chicago Tribune*, he worked for a Midwestern heirloom apple orchard. His first book, *Will It Waffle?: 53 Irresistible and Unexpected Recipes to Make in a Waffle Iron*, won praise from the *New York Times*, *People* magazine, and Food52. He lives in Montreal.